GrowerTalks
on
Retailing

Edited by John H. Saxtan

Ball Publishing

Batavia, Illinois USA

95-216

Ball Publishing
335 North River Street
P.O. Box 9
Batavia, Illinois 60510-0009 USA

Library of Congress Cataloging in Publication Data

GrowerTalks on retailing / edited by John H. Saxtan.
     p.   cm.
  Includes bibliographical references and index.
  ISBN 1-883052-03-3: $27.00
  1. Garden centers (Retail trade)—Management.
I. Saxtan, John H.
  SB454.6.G76   1994
  635.9'068'8—dc20   93-42987
                                                  CIP

Front cover: Alstroemeria (lower right), Agro-Plant B.V.,
           Aalsmeer, the Netherlands.
Back cover: Color bowl, PanAmerican Seed Co., West
           Chicago, Illinois.
           Retail entrance, Wilson Farms, Lexington,
           Massachusetts.

Contents

CHAPTER 3 Color Bowls and Containers

CHAPTER 4 Employee Management

CHAPTER 5 Customer Service

About the Authors

Neal Catapano is co-owner/grower at Catapano Farms, Southhold, Long Island, New York.

Douglas Green is owner of Simple Gifts Farm Greenhouses, Athens, Ontario, Canada.

Dave Hamlen is president of Hamlen's Garden Center, Swanton, Vermont.

Kim Hawks is co-owner of Niche Gardens, Chapel Hill, North Carolina.

Peter Konjoian is part-owner of Konjoian's Greenhouses, Andover, Massachusetts.

Roy A. Larson is professor of floriculture, North Carolina State University, Raleigh, North Carolina.

Julie A. Martens is former managing editor of *GrowerTalks* magazine.

Russell Miller is a former assistant editor at *GrowerTalks* magazine.

Dawn Nelson is a freelance writer and owner of a commercial video production company in Houston, Texas.

Mary Lu Parks is owner of Florascope Communications, Birmingham, Alabama.

Kathleen Pyle is associate editor of *GrowerTalks* magazine.

John H. Saxtan is a writer, editor and publisher from Naperville, Illinois.

Ivan C. Smith is president of Ivan Campbell Smith, Inc., a Lancaster, Ohio, consulting firm.

Steven and Suz Trusty, Trusty and Associates, Council Bluffs, Iowa, provide a variety of services to the horticultural industry.

C. Anne Whealy is the director of Proprietory Rights International, Roanoke, Texas.

Ann Turner Whitman is a horticultural writer in Bolton, Vermont.

Acknowledgments

Any book, particularly a collection of articles such as this, is the result of many people's efforts. Credits for this book go to editor John H. Saxtan, author, editor, contributing writer to *GrowerTalks,* and currently editor and publisher of a national telecommunications trade magazine, who took the compiled material, edited it, and turned it into a book; to Julie Martens, former managing editor of *GrowerTalks,* for originally conceiving the idea of a *GrowerTalks on Retailing,* as well as her work in writing many of the articles, and helping to select, compile and organize the material; to Bev Stelk, former editorial assistant, who gathered the articles, organized them for editing, and entered the material for editing; to Diane McCarthy, book production editor, who kept the project moving and handled the myriad details that go into producing a book; to Liza Sutherland, copy editor, who copy edited the material for style and content, checked for factual accuracy, and made sure commas were in their rightful places; and to all the authors and the people they interviewed, for writing and sharing solid, useful information about greenhouse retailing.

Introduction

Are You Being Served?

I think of myself as an "average" consumer when I visit retail greenhouses and garden centers. Until I read over the material in this book, however, I hadn't given much thought to what I liked or disliked about certain retail operations, or what my real expectations were. Now, however, I have a better idea of why I favor one place over another, and if it were to be summed up in two words, those words would be "customer service." Everything you do in retailing goes back to customer service in some way.

From physical layout to product mix, hours of operation, knowledgeable staff, advertising and even how you answer the phone, everything relates to serving the customer. If your space is arranged for pleasant viewing of products, easy access, good traffic flow, (not only in the aisles but also in the parking lot), quick checkout, and safety for non-greenhouse personnel (no tripping over hoses or losing a heel in gravel), you have thought of your customer.

If you're offering new and different classes as well as new varieties of plants, if your salespeople are courteous and knowledgeable, if your plants are clearly marked, you're not only giving yourself a competitive edge, you're giving the customer good reasons for having chosen your store.

How do you get into retailing? What are the differences from wholesaling? Will you have to build? Remodel? What have other growers done to be successful? These questions, and many others, are the reason for this book, and hopefully you will find most of the answers in these pages.

All of the material printed here originally appeared in *GrowerTalks* magazine over the past several years, but instead of just being reprinted articles, the material has been organized into seven major sections about retailing.

You'll find that when a particularly good idea in one chapter applies to the topic of another chapter, it appears in both places—you don't have to remember where you read that great idea or read through the entire book to get all the information you want on a particular subject.

If you are thinking about getting into retailing or expanding the retail operations of your greenhouse, we believe this book can help you find out what you want to know. Just remember to imagine yourself as a customer. Would you want to shop here? Would you want to buy this product? Are you being served?

—John H. Saxtan, editor

CHAPTER 1

Make Space for Retailing

Plan Garden Center Changes for Success[1]

by Steven and Suz Trusty

The time has come to get serious about a change. You want to start retailing for the first time or to expand into a full service garden center or to open a new location. All you must do is determine your needs and determine how to fill those needs. Simple to say; complex to enact.

Ernest Wertheim, landscape architect and garden center design specialist of Wertheim, van der Ploeg & Klemeyer, San Francisco, California, urges anyone contemplating growth or expansion to start with the basics. He and partner Frederick J. (Jack) Klemeyer Jr. jointly conduct Garden Center Design Seminars covering these basics. Participants come out of the seminar, not with a design, but with knowledge of what to consider in completing one.

Ask Questions That Make You Think

- First, define your operating philosophy—in writing. What type of business are you operating? Are you good? Why? Who are your customers and your competition? At what rate is your business now growing?

- Where do you want to be five years from now? Ten years? Will the anticipated expansion take you there? Will you be serving the same customers? Who are your potential customers? Will your competition change?

- Will competitors be entering the market? Keep tabs on happenings to investigate this possibility. Review plans filed with local boards and seek input from sources, such as sales representatives.

It's important to define these factors. Your operating philosophy will dictate the type of business you develop. It will influence the look of your building and the merchandise you stock.

Listen to Your Customers

Customers come to you because they like the way your business philosophy is expressed in operation—in appearance, quality, value, service, atmosphere or any combination of these. Keep the needs of these customers foremost in your planning.

Talk to them. Ask why they buy from you. Ask what products and services they would like to see you add. Find out what they like about your facility.

Build on your positives. If you are a wholesale grower planning to enter the retail arena, customers might enjoy browsing through the greenhouse and getting their plants direct from the source. Make sure your planning includes easy access to a designated retail greenhouse and allows you to control access to your production greenhouses without making your shoppers feel restricted.

Consider remodeling to accommodate customers who are on their lunch breaks or who stop by after work by adding paved parking areas and walkways, additional elevated benches, an express checkout line and covered outdoor display space.

The seminar emphasizes these variables. Each business is unique. There is no one magic formula. The changes you make must be developed for your business, operating in your locale, serving your market.

Be Systematic in Design Plans

Through the seminar, Wertheim and Klemeyer help you identify your current and future problems and help you find solutions. Your changes must be the best ones for your operation. Wertheim says, "Plan for maximum efficiency. The better we solve details, the more efficiently we operate."

Klemeyer suggests starting a looseleaf notebook. Jot down all ideas. Put in photos of operations you like and notes telling why. Prior to your site purchase or expansion, define building requirements; note sizes, shapes and building materials. Investigate ordinances and restrictions. Check out land prices.

It's best to design specifically by area what you want to accomplish by a remodeling or building program. Program for growth. Determine precisely what needs to be done.

Wertheim feels you should allow a minimum of one year from the start of the thought process before you are ready to begin any construction. As the business owner, planning and construction can consume approximately 50 percent of your time. You must also keep your business operating. Be prepared to assign up to 50 percent of your normal tasks to others during this planning and construction period.

Identify and Target Problems

Now analyze and define your current problems, and those perceived with your new location or remodeled building, as accurately and completely as possible. If you don't define the right problem, you won't reach the right solution. For each problem ask, How does this problem make itself evident?

"I need more parking" is a solution statement. A problem statement is, "My parking area is congested during busy times."

Develop problem statements for all problems. Others might be: My checkout area is congested. My cash flow has too many valleys and too few peaks. I have difficulty finding trained personnel. My outside bedding area often looks picked over. I don't receive telephone messages quickly.

Is there any correlation between problems? Will one be solved by solving the other? The idea here is to use lateral thinking to reach the real reason for the problem. Don't be limited by thinking in set patterns or simple solutions.

Possible Parking Problems

Parking congestion could be caused by inefficient checkout procedures that slow customer service, poorly defined lot entrances and exits, undefined traffic flow within the lot, employee use of parking areas, interference from loading company delivery vehicles, or poorly placed receiving areas. The solution to the real problem may not call for more parking area at all.

When there are a variety of potential solutions, think through the ramifications of each. Changes made in one area can affect the operations of another. More efficient parking can allow increased customer traffic, which may require different checkout arrangements.

Now think about the changes—why you want to make them and what you expect them to accomplish.

Define the Garden Center

Wertheim and Klemeyer refer to the "garden center" as the entire retail facility, including the retail outlet, display greenhouses, floral shop, shade houses, offices, storage and staging areas, shipping and receiving area, outside sales area, maintenance and any additional buildings, parking, landscaped show areas and undeveloped land. Retention and detention ponds may be required as part of the garden center.

Other segments of the business, such as production greenhouses, growing fields and design and sales offices, might also be located on the same site. Each area must fulfill its own function and interact effectively with all others.

Decide which elements you want to include. Translate each into a specific size. Now make a schematic plan, an initial idea concept, of these

3

elements. Your basic ideas can be expressed in these plans. Then, when you do the design development, you can assess the costs compared to the benefits.

Work Accurately and to Scale

Even picking up a few of the seminar details make planning so much more exact. Allow a minimum of 400 square feet of paved area per car. This will allow enough room to park and have the needed access drives. Additional space will be needed for landscaped areas or other extras.

Of every 1,000 square feet of inside retail display space, 30 to 32 percent will be available for actual display. The rest is taken up by aisles. This figure will seldom reach 35 percent, no matter how well you preplan.

The width of your aisles can vary somewhat with the size of your operation. It's desirable to allow room for two shopping carts to pass. Small operations could have 6-feet-wide main aisles, medium sized operations 8 feet and large ones 10 feet. Secondary aisles can become narrower the farther they are from the main flow of traffic. Anything less than 5 feet can be a tight squeeze.

Maintain a 60/40 relationship in your outside display area. Major aisles must be at least 8 feet wide. If you are using vehicles to place and retrieve

FIGURE 1. *Aisle widths in retail display areas can vary, but it's best to allow room for two shopping carts to pass. Photo taken at Graeber Gardens, Salinas, California.*

stock, allow a minimum of 12 feet. Check this against the actual turning radius of your equipment: forklifts, front end loaders and tractors and carts.

Plan Traffic Flow

The shopper's natural tendency is to turn to the right. Keep that in mind when planning your traffic flow. Remember you must entice the customer to shop. Avoid long stretches. Plan on something exciting at least every 100 feet to keep them moving through.

Wertheim says, "Display is like a stage, and the plants (or products) become the actors." Make sure the plants give a performance well rewarded by your customers' dollars.

Draw each section accurately to scale; cut them out. Move them around on a site plan also drawn to scale. It is most helpful in considering either expansion or a new site to get to this stage. It defines the basics of size and shape and lets you know how much and what type of area is required.

During this growth process, be it expansion, remodeling, or building, you are examining the feasibility of each option. Keep a close eye also on each option's relationship to your overall financing. Small sketch feasibility studies developed during each planning stage help tremendously in needs projections. When you face the projected dollar expenditures, you can quickly assume some basic alternative programs.

Successful Site Selection

- Much must be considered when selecting a site. What is the cost? Is the area big enough for future expansion? Will the land appreciate in value? How does it relate to your customer location? Will satellite locations accommodate people in other areas? What are the area's labor cost and availability?

- What is the shape of the site? What is the access to major roads and commuter traffic? Will your business be both visible and accessible? Where can entrances and exits be placed? Will zoning restrict their number? How about setback rules and sign restrictions?

- What is the water source? Will you need retention ponds? What is the topography? Will it limit options? Check with a soil engineer to ensure soil structure will support your buildings. Is there anything buried beneath the site? Are utilities readily available and economical? What is the surrounding area like? Are there neighbors who may raise objections to your center's equipment, noise or traffic?

- How attractive is the site? Will it appeal to your customers? Is there existing vegetation? Is it an asset or a drawback? Are there existing structures or roadways? Are they assets?

- What authorities must you deal with to develop this location—local, county and state boards, highway departments? Will local building codes and ordinances limit your choices? What plans must each group review and at what stage of development?

Each of these areas could be the source of tremendous problems that could add to your costs and slow your planning and construction.

Appraise All Options

Consider just the shape of the site. The shape directly affects the layout's efficiency. How much of the property will actually be usable? On a 400-foot by 600-foot site, with a 100-foot setback requirement, the differences in usable area go from 75 to 84 percent, depending on whether the 100-foot setback must be deducted from a 400-foot or 600-foot frontage. A 50-foot setback is not unusual.

Consider land costs plus the costs of improvements you must make in relation to your market area. Check land costs with three or more sources. Don't forget to factor in present and projected property taxes and any unusual costs. If the costs are appropriate, see if you can take an option on the land until you are ready to start building. If you must make an outright purchase, try to generate cash flow.

To Move or Stay

Expansion and rebuilding on your existing site can be a major disruption of current business and a great inconvenience to customers. All remodeling is not practical. Look again. You owe yourself thorough appraisal of all options.

Plan on working any construction around your existing business, especially remodeling. (The thought of this alone could be the deciding factor to move.) You may need to phase construction. This does cost more in the long run but may be the most feasible for effective operation.

Be sure to compare property costs, building financing or improvements, fixture costs and added inventory, and increased overhead with either option. Factor in benefits that will accrue, such as investment tax credits.

Project increased income. If you know the average dollar figure spent by customers, determine how many customers you will need at that dollar volume to equal the projected increase. Also figure your current annual dollar volume per square foot. Will expansion keep the relationship between these figures? Will the added room be adequate for the additional customers needed?

Remember that 50 to 60 percent of the retail sales volume is achieved in approximately six weeks. Are your projections realistic?

Presenting Your Case—to Lenders and Customers

Imagine Ernest Wertheim leaning forward and staring directly into your eyes or Jack Klemeyer rubbing his chin and tilting his head slightly to the side. Be prepared, here come the questions: Why are you doing this? How will this work? What happens if you have six weeks of rain or if you have none?

Give yourself enough ammunition to answer these questions, and defend your answers. Your banker may ask the same ones. Approach the bank early. Assemble an attractive and detailed presentation. Work closely with them.

Be sure to let your customers know what is happening. Include them in all steps of the process. Display a model showing the changes you will be making. Include a progress report in your monthly newsletter. Issue handouts explaining what will be happening next.

Train your staff to operate in the new facility or under the newly remodeled set-up. Cautions Wertheim, "Don't say please come back in three months when we get organized." When you are sure you are ready for the exposure, go all out on a big grand opening. Send invitations. Entice new customers as well as your regulars.

Changes are hard work. But if you've followed the guidelines of Wertheim, van der Ploeg & Klemeyer, you've planned for success.

To reach Ernest Wertheim and Frederick J. Klemeyer Jr., contact

Wertheim, van der Ploeg & Klemeyer,
2145 19th Avenue, #2,
San Francisco, California 94116,
(415) 664-0832.

Space—The Retailer's Frontier [2]

by Dave Hamlen

Several years ago I hired a consultant to look at our garden center and give us some ideas about our retail space use. I was astonished when he said he didn't know what business we were in. I had always prided myself on a neat, clean image for our store front and greenhouses.

We had a sign out front and product neatly displayed inside—a neat, clean business. Nothing wrong with neat and clean, but our customers couldn't see what we had to offer. White alyssum looked great massed inside the greenhouse, but sales doubled when we displayed alyssum near the entrance.

What Impression Does Your Business Give?

Some of your most effective selling space is in front of your business. Drive by your business as a customer would: Are you attracted by products, banners and flags? Does your business look fun, exciting and inviting? If not, then this is the first place to start work.

I've heard that light, color, sound and motion get attention. One retailer I know uses farm animals near the road to attract customers. Another retailer uses flashing lights to get attention for his ever-changing sign. But whatever way you use, it has to be in keeping with the business image you're trying to project.

Provide Good Parking

Once customers come into your business, they are likely to ask where to park their cars and how to enter your business. What kind of space are you providing for parking? Is it well defined? Relatively close to the front door? Is the surface clean and easy to walk on? (Don't forget women in high heels.) Do customers have enough room to turn their cars around?

I once installed a traffic island perpendicular to the entrance drive, causing traffic to slow down to navigate around the island. I prided myself on this traffic control and landscaped the island with large rocks and a variety of shrubs. Later, when we took the island out, I realized I had done it for my benefit, not the customers'. I don't know how many told me how glad they were to see the island gone.

Once you've shown people how to park, show them how to enter your business. The entrance should be wide enough for carts and people to pass through. It shouldn't be so wide, however, that someone tries to make a drive-up out of the entry. Eight to 12 feet is usually wide enough.

Use Entry Space for Promotions

Your entry space is valuable, too. Its space will be noticed more than any other on your property. We like to locate some of our promotions here. A round wire spool table placed in the entry middle with a promotion sitting on top works well. The round table allows customers to move easily around it, while making a point.

Even though this is valuable space, don't put your most valuable product here. If the item at your entry point is too pricey, you'll be labeled as expensive and from then on, you'll have to discount a lot of merchandise to convince the customer you price fairly. Remember, "you get only one chance to make a good first impression."

Customers Need Direction

Once your customers are inside your front door, lead them where you want them to go, either directly or indirectly. One retailer I know designed his

FIGURE 2. *Colorful displays by your entrance will attract attention and paying customers. Photo taken at Wilson Farms, Lexington, Massachusetts.*

store so that customers move through the store in a one-way fashion. This is direct leading.

Using lights, color, sound or motion is indirect leading. The same retailer who uses one-way store traffic also has animated displays to lead customers into other retail space.

Less Is More

Retailers are never quite sure about how much product to display. More is not always better. We retail out of one greenhouse and grow in the other eight greenhouses. We never display more than 10 to 15 percent of all our crops at one time. We do this for several reasons. Our retail greenhouse has 4- to 6-foot-wide aisles for easy customer circulation, and we're able to keep our best plants in front of the customer.

The retail store is another area where you don't have to display all you have. If your store is small like ours, you can't show 20 of the same product. A display of three to five may be all the room you have. You may need someone to keep an eye on restocking, but it will be an efficient space use.

As a small business enterprise owner, don't be influenced by the mass merchandiser. They try to display as much product as possible, and they'll stock it as high as they can, utilizing costly space. But their type of operation lacks the character yours has.

Use Wall Space to Sell

Make sure your customers can easily see over your displays so that they are attracted to the next display. They also will see wall displays where product can be displayed from the knee to the shoulders. Extra product can be stacked on the floor under the wall shelves. Space above the top shelves can be used for pictures or banners.

This is a good area to show off pictures of your customers' gardens or plants. If you do landscaping, show people the quality of your work. This is all valuable selling space, only you're selling ideas here and not product.

Inspire Your Customers

Customers want to be inspired by seeing what they can do with their own homes and yards. Pictures and displays can help, as do informational sheets or brochures. Next to the pots and potting soil, show how pots can be attractively grouped with plant varieties. If one of your customers has success with a certain fertilizer, ask him to bring in a picture of the plant or plants and display it with the fertilizer.

It's also important to let your customers know you appreciate them. Each December we seem to have more store than product, so we take one wall and create a Christmas scene. This uses store space and creates a special feeling for our customers.

Convenient Checkouts

The best space for the checkout counter is near the entry/exit point. We use one register near the front door and a second in a shed near the parking lot entry. The second register is used during busy times to keep lines short. It's important for customers to pay for their purchases and leave your retail space when they're ready. People may spend hours shopping; however, when they're ready to leave, they don't want to stand in line.

Conquering your retail space can give you happier customers and more profit. When you see sales increasing, you'll know you're successfully using your retail space.

To Park or Not to Park:
the Springtime Challenge[3]

by Dave Hamlen

How customer-friendly is your parking lot? It's true that a parking lot is just a place for people to park their cars while visiting your business. But are you missing sales because people can't find a place to park? Are you losing business because your customers were so frustrated trying to park they lost their real objective for stopping?

After a busy weekend I would see some of our customers at the local grocery store. One thing they'd tell me was, "I tried to stop at your place this weekend, but there was no place to park." This didn't bother me too much. We'd had a busy weekend; a lot of money went into the register. What was one lost sale?

What I should have realized was that they probably weren't the only ones who couldn't drive in. We were losing customers because of a too-crowded parking lot. Rather than priding myself on "packing them in" on a busy weekend, I should have been concerned about how I could have attracted the customers who passed by.

Creating More Parking

- **Build a bigger lot.** One way to allow for more parking is to increase the parking lot's size. This can help if you have space available, but it isn't always possible where land is at a premium.

- **Hire a traffic cop.** One solution that helped our parking situation was to hire a deputy sheriff on weekends during busy hours. Now when a customer sees a uniformed person at our entrance directing

11

traffic, they're on their best behavior. Instead of parking where they please—taking two or three parking spaces—they're directed to occupy one space. The officer's presence creates an orderly parking lot—customers aren't irritated from driving into a bottleneck. We soon realized this had a very positive influence on our parking situation.

Not only did the officer directing traffic near the road allow more people to enter, but the flashing blue light on his car slowed motorists down. It made them think there must be something "big" going on here. The flashing light on the officer's car can be very effective if you're a retailer located on a busy highway. Slowing people down allows them to see and smell the roses at your establishment.

- **Load orders in drive-up areas.** It's advantageous to load bulky customer purchases away from the parking lot. On a busy selling day this can provide extra parking space, resulting in more sales. If the customer with a large order can pull directly up to the greenhouse, it will save you loading time. Nursery stock, peat moss, bark mulches and other bulky items are best loaded in drive-up areas. Remember, you want your parking lot to look busy but approachable to potential shoppers.

- **Keep the lot full.** A full or almost full parking lot makes a business look exciting. Providing people can get in, they want to know what all the excitement is about—they don't want to miss out on something special. One car in a parking lot doesn't create excitement.

  One way to create parking lot excitement is to use the vehicles on hand. During not-so-busy times, have employees park in customer spaces. It's best not to have designated employee parking. Encourage employees to park in different spots so that regular passersby don't see the same vehicles in the same places.

  I know of one garden center owner who has threatened to bring in some junk cars to make his parking lot look full. Automobile dealers have known about parking lot display for some time. Although their inventory may not change, they keep moving their vehicles. This gives the passerby the excitement of a change and makes a business look like something's happening.

- **Keep the entrance open.** A customer entering your business wants to park as close to the front door as possible. You shouldn't deny them this privilege, but don't allow them to monopolize your entrance. We found people would park so close to the front door that our store entrance became congested.

We installed no-parking signs, but these weren't noticed. So we placed four one-half whiskey barrels in front of the entrance and planted them with various combinations of annuals. That solved the parking problem plus helped sell annuals and whiskey barrels.

- **Calculate space needs.** How much space should you allow for each customer's car? If your parking lot is paved with parking lines, they should be approximately 9 feet wide by 20 feet long. If your lot isn't paved, then you want to allow a 10- to 12-foot width per car. A rough guide to use is plan on 400 square feet per car.

  To allow customers to back out of their parking spaces, make sure they have 40 feet of length, or twice the length of the parking space. This space shouldn't conflict with drive-through space. With parking lot space, more is definitely better.

- **Remember handicapped access.** In planning your parking lot, be sure to allow space for the handicapped. To find out more information about accommodating the handicapped, contact the

  Office on the Americans with Disabilities Act,
  Civil Rights Division,
  U.S. Department of Justice,
  P.O. Box 66118, Washington, D.C.
  20035-6118
  (202) 514-0301

- **Paved vs. non-paved surfaces.** The parking lot surface may not be as important as you think. Quite often, greenhouses and nurseries feel they need a paved parking lot. Although pavement is nice, when we asked customers which surface they preferred, they didn't say. As long as the surface was easy to walk on, not muddy or slippery, with relatively few potholes, they were content.

  One customer referred to the paved parking lot as the "shopping mall look." He felt when people come to a greenhouse or garden center, they're coming to the farm and expect to get a little dirty. But this doesn't mean that we need to display the greenhouse compost pile near the front door or even in sight, either.

- **Deal with non-customers positively.** The number of people who use our parking lot as a turnaround often amazes me. Perhaps it's because of a garden center parking lot's size. Whatever the reason, these people are attracted to our store because we conveniently meet their need to navigate in another direction. Rather than becoming angry at these parking lot abusers, we have a highly visible banner or sign telling about our business.

Banners like "Protect your Plants for Winter," "Fall Is for Plant-ing," "Plant Spring Bulbs," "Memorial Day Color" and "New Nursery Stock" can acquaint the passerby with your business. Everyone who enters your store property is a potential customer. If you can't sell them something at that instant, then they should at least know about it for the future.

Turn Passersby to Customers

I began to realize parking's importance when we surveyed our customers several years ago. One question we asked our customers was why they stopped in. Sixty-four percent answered "because they were passing by." Since there has to be available parking space, I felt it should be attractive, too.

Now on busy weekends, a deputy sheriff helps keep the parking lot available for maximum usage. Rerouting truck traffic and customer pickups of bulky items has freed up space for prospective customers. By providing enough parking space per customer and a pleasing parking lot surface, you can entice customers to buy.

It's far better that we ask ourselves how can we accommodate more customers in the parking lot, than hear as Shakespeare in a mad moment might have said, "Alas, poor Hamlen, I might have stopped if only you had given me enough parking space."

Adding Retail Space[4]

by Russell Miller

The original retail garden center at Busy Bee, Glenwood, Illinois, is a 15,000-square-foot X.S. Smith greenhouse covered with double poly. A 10,000-square-foot Campbell O'Brien greenhouse was purchased and erected by the Busy Bee staff. It's built without sidewalls so drive-by customers on busy Halsted Street can catch a glimpse of spectacular spring-through-fall color.

This open-ended greenhouse is covered with milky white double-poly to protect crops and customers from the weather. It allows for comfortable shopping, rain or shine. When the temperature approached freezing one spring night, the Fasels [owners of the business] simply hung poly down the sides of the structure and no plants were lost, even though it ended up snowing the next morning.

"It's one of the best additions we ever made to the retail side of the business," Bob Fasel says. "It was inexpensive to build, and it increased customer traffic. We moved 22,000 flats of annuals through it this spring.

That's in addition to what we sold through our 24,000-square-foot garden center and retail shop.

Give Them Plenty to Choose From

"During the spring we average 3,000 to 3,500 flats of annuals and 600 to 700 baskets on hand every day for retail. We like to cater to the customers, giving them a lot to choose from. On a busy day we can do $60,000 to $70,000 in retail sales. It's a madhouse at times. We have about 80 employees dealing with the customers on a one-to-one basis almost all the time in the spring."

Outside the retail center, estimated to contain more than $1 million in plants, hardgoods and other products, are 150 car parking spaces. Customers enter the garden center, florist and gift shop by passing through a large nursery and statuary area first. Signage is everywhere. Concrete walkways make it easier for the customers to push shopping carts, which help sell more plants.

Inside the 9,000-square-foot gift "village" are high-quality gifts, everything from $1 knickknacks to $500 vases and $200 handmade leather purses. The inventory amounts to over $500,000.

They have more than 200 gift suppliers. Some gifts are imported, others are unique, rare American-made products. Expensive lawn chair and patio sets grace one room, and there's an extensive greeting card section near a full-service floral shop.

Silk, Dried Flowers Sell Well

Busy Bee also does a profitable silk and artificial plant business—nearly $100,000 worth of stock. "Silk plants are really taking off," Jim says. Placing live plants intermixed with silk plants in the retail center increases the sales of both, he adds. They also do a profitable retail dried flower business using their own designers.

Basically, Busy Bee is a one-stop shopping center—there's obviously something here for everyone, be it plants or gifts. Both help sell the other.

Making a Long-term Investment in Retail [5]

by Julie A. Martens

Longfellow's, Manchester, Maine, is a retail garden center that caters to customers. As much of the product as possible is covered, everything is accessible with wide, 4-foot aisles, plants are displayed at convenient

FIGURE 3. *For customer convenience, make sure directions to a checkout are clearly marked. Photo taken at Longfellow's, Manchester, Maine.*

heights, and signage serves to direct and educate. Staff members know that customer interaction is the most important aspect of their jobs.

"I stress to our staff that if you have a hose in your hand, then, to customers, you're an expert," Scott Longfellow says. "Everyone here knows that saying, 'I don't know' is the best response—instead of making something up. Then they know to find someone who knows an answer."

We Offer Variety

Being customer-oriented means offering variety and selection, up to as many as 45 varieties each of petunias and impatiens. Scott sees high variety numbers as "difficult but interesting." It also sets the business apart from chain stores, who may offer only four petunia varieties.

The main retail area at Longfellow's is a Dynaglass-covered, 5,600-square-foot post and beam structure, like a barn without sides. The total investment in the structure, built in 1987, was about $1.43 per square foot for everything except the Dynaglass.

The display area has hanging baskets along the outside edge and at many support posts. Benches are 3- by 12-feet and arranged at angles, so customers can reach all product on a bench. The floor is bark-covered, and there are benches in a display area at one end of the building. The whole effect is very open and airy, very garden-oriented.

Moving Plants—and More—at a One-Stop-Shopping Retail Center[6]

by Julie A. Martens

What has tour buses in the parking lot, floral dinnerware in the gift department and purple all over? It's Bachman's in Minneapolis, Minnesota, a top-of-the-line retailing operation that's been sending out flowers and floral-related items in their signature color—purple—since the 1930s.

The operation at 6010 Lyndale Avenue in south Minneapolis is a floral and garden complex, complete with retail florist services, a floral gift department, nursery, landscaping and interiorscaping divisions, hardgoods area and retail greenhouses. There's also 60,000 square feet of growing area at the site, along with a floral supply warehouse and a distribution center.

Bachman's knows the flower and plant market, with 15 full-service floral stores, three garden and landscaping centers and 16 Flowers By Bachman's stores—free-standing kiosks selling flowers, plants and gifts in supermarkets and shopping malls—all located throughout Minnesota. Growing for the various operations takes place on 438 acres in Lakeville, Minnesota.

But it's the retail store on Lyndale that has drawn local schools, garden clubs and civic organizations by the bus load to take a look behind the scenes of retail growing. "The trick to keeping people interested is to do exciting things," says Todd Bachman, a former company executive. From the retail areas to the display greenhouses, excitement is everywhere.

Welcoming Customers with Warmth

When customers enter Bachman's, they step into a light-filled, airy atrium, complete with coffee and cold drinks. Displays in the atrium change with the four seasons, with an additional holiday display set up at Christmas. "We use the atrium as our formal greeting area," Todd explains. "Customers stop here for a break—there are refreshments and a place to sit. It's perfect for socializing or gathering a group."

17

From the atrium, shoppers move into either the retail greenhouses or the 20,000 square feet of retail display space. It's here that fresh flowers, silks, dried flowers and gift items fill floor and wall space. Each department flows into the next, making access convenient for both the first-time shopper and Bachman's "regulars."

"All of our stores are designed so displays are easily changed," Todd says. "We use a lot of blocks and mobile units that are lightweight." The first retail area off the atrium houses different displays throughout the year—from silks to wicker to a bucket floral shop for Mother's Day.

Fresh cut flower sales take place at one end of the showroom, with a self-serve cooler sporting bunches of mixed or single stem flowers. These floral bunches are priced to be affordable and packaged to be convenient.

We Go for Quality

Bachman's sources cuts from all over the world, including domestic production. "We're always looking for what's new and different," Todd explains, "but, above all, we go for quality." All stems are treated with silver thiosulfate and placed in floral preservative to ensure longest vase life.

For more formal arrangements, customers can take advantage of the FTD wire service features or consult with the salespeople for individually designed floral pieces. One item that's popular is the floral "treat yourself" cart. "This idea reminds us of the flower carts used in open markets," Todd says. "Each week we feature a small blooming plant or fresh flowers. It's our way of getting more flowers into more people's homes."

The Retail Greenhouse

A 23,000-square-foot display space offers a wide selection of plants in a variety of sizes and price points in the retail greenhouse area. The philosophy behind plant sales is to encourage customers to use plants for themselves, as well as for gifts. The philosophy again emphasizes Bachman's campaign for getting more flowers in people's lives.

The retail displays change with the seasons, with special foliage promotions twice a year. Weekly specials offer something for either the beginning or experienced gardener. "We use the display area to highlight new ways to use plants," Todd explains. "Last spring, for instance, we featured the new European-type garden, with foliage plants and flowers potted together and held in a wicker basket."

In spring, mobiles and whirligigs add color and movement to the plant displays. Again, the presence of purple is strong, this time in a 55-gallon fertilizer drum. Customers bring their own containers and fill them for free with Bachman's in-house fertilizer.

Ready for Questions

Salespeople are readily available for questions, and there's an information booth where planting demonstrations and plant care information is offered as printed material or as responses from the knowledgeable staff members. The retail greenhouse is a Lord and Burnham glass structure, featuring hanging baskets, mixed planters, bedding plants and water lilies.

The retail plant area wraps around the garden center nursery display, so customers see outdoor plant offerings as they walk through the home and hardgood areas. Casual furniture for patios and decks is a popular item, reflecting Bachman's efforts to gear business specifically to their customers' living styles.

Hardgoods include everything from irrigation systems and sprayers to lawn mowers and planters. Bachman's features its private label fertilizer and indoor plant care products prominently, giving customers access to some of their growing "secrets."

Molbak's of Seattle:
We Are Retail Driven [7]

by Russell Miller

Molbak's Greenhouse in Woodinville, Washington, a few miles northeast of Seattle, didn't have much more than 15,000 square feet of glass-covered greenhouses when Egon and Laina Molbak purchased the property in 1956. Today, it's not only one of the largest retail garden centers in the Pacific Northwest, it's also one of the country's most outstanding as well.

"Back then, we had visions of Molbak's becoming a sizable business, but we didn't expect to become retailers, and we didn't expect Molbak's to become as diversified as it is today," Egon says. "We began as wholesalers and then began retailing on a seasonal basis in 1957. In the mid-1960s, we analyzed the possibility of going into year-round retail sales and in 1968, we saw that it was going to be successful, so we began retailing year-round."

In 1970, Molbak's bulldozed down and rebuilt about 75 percent of the original greenhouses. Also added was 10,500 square feet of retail greenhouses, a parking lot and additional support structures. "From there it kept growing," Egon says. "Today retailing accounts for about 85 percent of our sales, and we have over 120,000 square feet of indoor and outdoor display areas."

Molbak's: the Destination Point

Molbak's is the connoisseur's garden center—a one-stop shopping center where customers can find the widest selection of plants and hard goods in the region. This is a "destination point" for many consumers and tourists alike, as Molbak's is listed in the Seattle visitor's guide as one place people have to see. "We aren't a neighborhood business," Egon adds. "People come and spend half a day here."

Over the years they have added a 1,800-square-foot conservatory filled with tropical plants and an aviary with exotic birds. Then came a 2,500-square-foot courtyard, adjoining the conservatory, and an espresso bar, where customers can enjoy a cup of gourmet coffee while seated in a forest of foliage and color, listening to classical music.

Statuary fountains and large, colorfully decorated plantings are found inside the garden center. Flowerbeds surround the business outside giving Molbak's retail greenhouses a park-like environment.

A Plant Supermarket[8]

by Russell Miller

Steve Hall of Wayne, Nebraska, believes quality, not price, is the best reason customers should come to your retail greenhouse. At The Wayne Greenhouse and Plant Market, quality sells the product. "You never have to worry about the competition if you can beat them on quality," he says. "If you have quality plants, you can pick your price."

The population of Wayne is about 5,200, yet it's one of the largest communities in northeastern Nebraska. "The population of Nebraska is about 1½ million, so there are not a lot of customers to attract," Steve says. "We do everything we can to get customers and then get them back again and again."

The business has two locations: a flower shop and glass-covered green-house in Wayne and The Wayne Greenhouse Plant Market, an 11,000-square-foot Stuppy greenhouse built in 1983, one mile east on the outskirts of Wayne.

The original Wayne Greenhouse is used for both retailing and growing cut flowers. The greenhouse also supplements the crops grown for retail at The Plant Market, where several double-inflated poly hoop houses are also in use to grow bedding plants and pot crops for retail and wholesale.

Stuppy-built for Comfort

The Plant Market's Stuppy greenhouse was built in 1983 and covered with Polygal. It has a concrete floor with buried heat and aisles wide enough so that customers can easily wheel grocery carts, modified to hold more plants. The greenhouse has a black thermal blanket and 50 percent white shade cloth which, when combined with pads and fans and air conditioning, provides customer comfort in summer. It's a supermarket of plants.

"We have ladies in dresses and high heels and men in suits coming in here after church on Sundays. We want them to be as comfortable as possible. We want them to stay. The longer they stay, the more they buy. People appreciate the comfort; it's one of the reasons they shop here." The greenhouse is kept spotless, the floor is swept and the benches are kept clean—another reason why customers, some driving for 100 miles or more, come to Plant Market.

Poly benches in the greenhouse can be easily repositioned because they are laid on sawhorses made of rebar. Steve can quickly redesign the floor layout for colorful displays and to accommodate seasonal fluctuations in crop numbers.

Creating a Special Look[9]

by Julie A. Martens

Driving west on Maryland's Route 40 brings you into the northern Appalachian Mountains and the small town of Frostburg, Maryland. One of the businesses, Harvey's Florist and Greenhouse, was established in 1930 and currently operates out of a renovated blue Victorian-style home on the east side of town.

Owner Penny Price bought Harvey's in 1984, five years after working as a full-time floral designer. "I didn't know anything about growing," Penny admits, "so for the first 1½ years Bob Wilson, the previous owner, taught me."

A retail area showcases dried flowers, silks and gift items with a floral or Victorian motif. "I'm trying to create a sort of floral theme park," explains Penny, "where people look forward to coming in and looking around. If they decide to buy something, great."

Rebuilding a Business

A year after Penny took over at Harvey's, she began remodeling the onsite house and greenhouses. It was a family affair from the start as her father handled the carpentry jobs, her brother developed the blueprints and laid stone, and her mother helped in the shop.

Feeling saturated with the country look that's so trendy, Penny chose a Victorian design. "I wanted something more whimsical, that complements the flower shop," Penny explains. "The design also had to be something that wouldn't go out of style." The final product includes living quarters above the retail shop and design areas and 4,800 square feet of production greenhouses.

Original structures at Harvey's were glass and steel frame greenhouses with cypress supports. Penny is gradually replacing the glass with Polygal to save on heating costs. Bench space is doubled with two-tiered benches, which will soon be outfitted with drip tube irrigation.

Ideas That Ring Up Sales[10]

by Steven and Suz Trusty

Here are some good ideas and solutions to problems that we've seen or heard about over the years. We hope you'll find something that you can put to use.

- From the outside sales yard of a Florida nursery outlet:

  The owners removed 3 inches of soil from the plant display sections between paved walkways and added coarse rock to bring the level of the section to just below that of the surrounding walkways.

  The rock was covered with a layer of geotextile material extended down to the soil level at the edges of the paving. Container plants were placed on top. This eliminated soil wash onto the walks and allowed excess water to drain away.

- From a Florida plant outlet serving a retirement community:

  All walkways were paved. Most plants were displayed on benches or raised platforms.

  Carts provided for do-it-yourself plant selection were only slightly lower than the benches. Each cart had an extended handle that stayed upright and was sturdy enough to lean on.

  "Bulk" packaging was smaller, usually 10 pounds or less, for easier at-home handling.

CHAPTER 2

Plan Your Product Mix

Colorful and Uncommon[1]

by Julie A. Martens

While the nation's retail outlets are feeling the pinch of recession-weary consumers, Oscar and Amy Cross, owners of Hilltop Farm in Ash Grove, Missouri, had customers who were spending 25 percent more on average in 1992 than in 1991. Hilltop Farm specializes in propagating, growing and retailing the unusual and exotic. The Crosses decided to go "full steam ahead" with variety in 1992, despite a sluggish national economy.

Their strategy worked, which left the weather as their major sales hindrance. "We've had a lot of days where it's not raining, but the air is heavy and wet," Oscar explains. "Even that keeps people away."

Strictly a Garden Center

Hilltop sells a little bit of everything—herbs, hanging baskets, annuals, garden mums and perennials. They also specialize in orchids and cyclamen during the winter months, completely avoiding poinsettias. "We grew excellent poinsettia crops for three years and only broke even," Oscar says. "We like plants, but we're not growing them to give them away."

The retail business is open regular hours April 1 to July 1. "We're a garden center in the strictest sense of the word," Oscar explains. "We don't sell trees, shrubs, gadgets or seed. We just sell plants."

Exotic Product Mix

Customers mostly come to Hilltop looking for things that are colorful and uncommon. For the Crosses, "exotic" doesn't refer to bougainvillea, hibiscus or mandevilla. Instead, exotics include leptosiphon, asarina, diascia or one of 200 varieties of hens and chicks. Other specialty items are "pretty pots," a 1- or 2-gallon pot of perennial color, like lythrum or garden phlox, and strawberry jars with violas or begonias.

Where do the Crosses find their plant material? "We take buying trips each year, and we visit trial grounds. We beat the bushes." Oscar feels strongly that the "really neat plants are in some little old lady's backyard" and are not coming from commercial breeders. "The last thing we need is a new petunia series. The breeders should concentrate on developing truly new material—like pink torenia, which, by the way, we were selling before it was commercially available—and improving existing, garden-proven lines."

Unique and New [2]

by Julie A. Martens

LaCrosse Floral, located in LaCrosse, Wisconsin, is a fourth generation family business with roughly a 75-25 split between retail and wholesale business. John Zoerb's grandfather started in the business in 1907, and today John and his children, Linda and Kevin, continue the legacy.

The business has a retail greenhouse, wholesale production, an interiorscape "plantscape" division and a full-service floral shop. The majority of greenhouse production retails through LaCrosse Floral's retail greenhouse; the remainder sells through local rural flower shops.

What sells well at LaCrosse Floral? Topiaries, bromeliads, potted hibiscus—"anything that's perceived as unique and new," according to Linda. Very hot items for Valentine's Day and Secretaries' Day are 4-inch African violets in a plastic bubble (from Dandy Enterprises, Wesley Chapel, Florida) and European dish gardens with bulbs.

Defining a Crop Mix

John Zoerb points out the two greatest challenges facing the family business: keeping a strong and growing customer base and competing with the ever-increasing floral outlets. How does LaCrosse plan to tackle these issues? By defining a niche. "We can't beat most of our competitors on price, so we go for quality, service and new items. We carry a unique cross-section of product for our customers to choose from," John says.

The crop mix at LaCrosse Floral includes Easter lilies, spring bedding and geraniums, pot mums, kalanchoes, cyclamen, poinsettias and a year-round supply of foliage and all Holland bulbs. John says. "Peony and poppy roots sell extremely well in the fall." LaCrosse arranges its perennials by height and uses a four-page info sheet with varieties, plant height and bloom time (arranged in a bar graph) to help customers make informed buying decisions.

Customers are interested in items they believe are different or new. To fit that bill, LaCrosse has offered tillandsia, hybrid foliage and traditional plants in unusual sizes—like "Jumbo" African violets in 6-inch pots, Granger Hybrid violets, Columbus, Ohio, and bonsai plants from the

Bonsai Company in Dayton, Ohio. Their next selection of "new" crops will be fresh cut freesia and Asiatic lilies. "The first year we grew freesia on a small scale, it went gangbusters," John says.

Following the Trends [3]

by Kathleen Pyle

In the 14 years Joel Schrock's owned Heinz Brothers Greenhouses in St. Charles, Illinois, he's made the transition from a wholesale operation to a full-service retail garden center. Today Heinz Brothers, located on Highway 64 in a rapidly developing area about 50 miles from Chicago, continues to draw customers from a wide radius.

Heinz Brothers' Varieties

Customers don't shop at Heinz Brothers because of discount prices—its prices are the highest in the local market. People come to Heinz Brothers to find variety and the unusual. In a recent year hanging baskets of "oddball" items such as Blue Wonder scaevola, russelia, lysimachia and dwarf chenille rushed out the door. Continuing to enlarge this retailing niche, Joel and Bob Bailey, general manager, contemplate hiring a contract grower to extend the garden center's growing space at an off-site location.

They also plan to produce crops in hard-to-locate sizes that will bring a maximum dollar return per square inch of space invested. An example is the 12-inch hanging basket zonal geraniums available at the garden center for a premium price. Most customers choose to immediately transplant these geraniums into the ground, but they're willing to pay the higher price for the right size.

Play to the Trends

With the increasing popularity of container gardening, Heinz Brothers' sales staff is promoting unusual container planting ideas, such as growing cannas in pots or cultivating green beans in containers for foliar effects. Catering to other new trends in consumer interest, Heinz Brothers sold water gardening products in 1992 for the first time. Bob reports these items have moved well.

On the other hand, over-anticipating demand can be costly. Bob is considering reducing perennial production by 10 percent. A 30-year veteran of the nursery industry, Bob's seen a cycle in perennials' popularity. "I'd like to test the trend," he says. "Perennials were a big thing in the 1960s and are now, but they're a rollercoaster probably headed toward a downhill slide."

FIGURE 4. *With container gardening gaining in popularity, retailers find that stocking a variety of supplies appeals to customers. Photo taken at Homewood Nursery, Raleigh, North Carolina.*

Although yarrow, hostas and daylilies are racking up impressive sales, Bob believes the average customers' interest in perennials will wane as they discover how transient the color impact is. Today's amateur home gardeners buy with three thoughts in mind: instant color, long-term color and low maintenance. Bailey tries to persuade Heinz Brothers' customers to plant a mixture of annuals and perennials so they'll only have to partially replant yearly for constant color.

Mixing Hardgoods and Service [4]

by Peter Konjoian

1990 was the 30th anniversary of my family's business, Konjoian's Greenhouses in Andover, Massachusetts. One aspect of our business philosophy that has never changed has been our approach to customer service. Give the best service possible. Period. No ifs, ands or buts about it.

High Tech Has Hit Horticulture

I believe we have an obligation to educate our customers so that they may experience greater success with our products. In my many garden club presentations and radio shows I spend time explaining the statement, "High tech has hit horticulture."

Several systems that we have installed in our commercial range are adaptable to the home landscape. We offer an automatic drip system to go with our hanging plants and container plants. This is a scaled down version of the irrigation system that we use in production and revolves around a common lamppost timer that we wire into a control board. The power behind the statement, "You will never have to water your hanging plant by hand," is realized by every customer who buys the system.

We are also working on a home version of constant feed. The smallest size Dosatron injector is great for this application. Tied into our drip system, we now can make the statement, "You will never have to water or fertilize your hanging plant by hand."

Automating Landscape Tasks

Offering these systems to help automate our customers' landscape tasks has been very well received. It is true that today's consumers have less time for boring tasks such as watering and fertilizing. Freeing up some of that time allows them to plant more flower and vegetable gardens, enjoy their homes more and spend less time cutting the grass—because they keep expanding their gardens.

Several years ago we invested in a soil mixing/pasteurizing system. We have always been more comfortable with our own soil-based mix and can now use state-of-the-art equipment to handle it properly.

An interesting and profit-generating spinoff to this project was to package and sell our mix to consumers. We had bags printed with "Konjoian's Professional Potting Soil" and a bit of information on them, purchased a heat sealer, and now we spend a few weekends in January bagging up a year's supply of potting soil instead of skiing.

Our customers have complete confidence in our mix. It seems that they have had bad experiences with some of the department store bargain brands they have used previously. Profits from this project are helping to pay for the soil equipment.

Herbs and Everlastings [5]

by Julie A. Martens

Driving east along state highway 35 in central Ohio around Labor Day, motorists are guaranteed a spectacular show of color on the south side of the road. The 10- to 12-acre display is the outdoor everlastings field production at Patchwork Gardens in Washington Court House.

Allen and Barbara Wilt are the head of this family-owned-and-operated business. Patchwork specializes in herbs and everlastings. "We've seen steady increases in sales every year," Allen says. "We're finding more and more customers who are definitely interested in dried flowers and cooking with herbs."

Sixty percent of the business at Patchwork Gardens is done through retail sales—herbs, everlastings, bedding plants, perennials—drawing from a customer base within a 75-mile radius. Wholesaling combination wicker baskets and bedding plants comprises the remainder of the business, with accounts at Kroger food stores from Toledo to West Virginia.

Marketing Year-Round with Herbs, Everlastings

Labor Day weekend is typically the peak color time for the everlastings in the field, and the Wilts host a Fall Open House the following Saturday for customers. "Last year, 800 people came in the course of the day," Barbara explains. "We take folks on a tour of the flower fields and drying barns and serve them a dinner of soup beans and tenderloin. It's a great family outing that brings good business for us."

Following the Fall Open House, family members harvest the fields and fill the drying barns. As the flowers dry, family members begin making dried flower wreaths and arrangements, which are featured in a 23,000-square-foot dried flowers and crafts display in retail greenhouse throughout November and December. A Christmas Open House marks the end of holiday everlastings sales.

The third annual open house is the Spring Herb and Everlastings Day, the first Saturday in May. This event features herbs, offering customers herbal teas, cookies, breads and recipes. Special speakers—often family members—offer seminars on cooking with herbs.

Herbs are available for sale, along with dried everlastings. "We're preparing the fields at this time," Jeff Wilt, grower, explains, "so people can see the everlastings from start to finish."

Plant Display Is Key

Showing customers how to use their plant products is a key element of the successful business at Patchwork Gardens. From everlastings arrangements to wreaths to herbal cooking, the family emphasizes product use to make sales.

Display gardens add to Patchwork's marketing tools, featuring an herb garden, perennial beds and bedding plants. A variety of wicker basket planter designs also offers customers planting ideas, using combinations of bedding plants, herbs and vegetables.

"Our basket line is very popular," Jeff says. "We do custom plantings for customers who return their baskets year after year. It's a steady business." The Wilts' primary basket supply comes from a basket maker in Kentucky, although they also use some wicker from China. The baskets are a popular item on the wholesale side of the business, with deliveries made in retrofitted hog trailers with three to four decks for baskets.

From bedding plant baskets to floral everlasting wreaths to herb bread, Patchwork Gardens offers both retail and wholesale customers a variety of products—well-labeled, well-promoted and well-displayed. The Wilts diversified their family farm to include flower production and have found their niche in specialty products.

FIGURE 5. *Stocking a plentiful supply of wicker baskets can give customers planting ideas and add variety to your product mix. Photo taken at Johnston the Florist, North Huntington, Pennsylvania.*

Georgia Perennials: a Retail Success [6]

by Julie A. Martens

Ten years ago in 1983 Goodness Grows Inc. in Lexington, Georgia, started producing perennials for wholesale, at a time when there were no large southern perennial growers. "People said you just couldn't grow perennials in the South," Rick Berry, co-owner, remembers.

Today production at Goodness Grows covers 7 acres, and only two-thirds of the perennials sell wholesale (to independent garden centers and landscapers from North Carolina to Tennessee to Alabama). The other third of production sells retail at the production site and by mail order.

Go for the Consumers

Rick and his partner Marc Richardson are pushing for more sales at the retail level. "Retail is the market that puts us in touch with consumers," Rick says. "And that's the best market for any grower."

Rick and Marc plan to build retail sales by increasing the product mix. "Mail order sales are a logical way to expand our business," Rick explans. "Once one of our gardening customers put our catalog onto the Prodigy home computer network, and mail orders increased overnight." For even more consumer-level exposure, they have also placed their catalog on file with botanical garden libraries in the Southeast.

Product Mix

The product mix at Goodness Grows includes perennials, flowering shrubs (a product area consumers are currently very interested in), trees, shade and sun loving native wildflowers and unusual annuals, like larkspur or cleome.

When Rick and Marc started growing perennials, they set a standard for container production of perennials rather than follow standards used for field production. Field producers have limited sales windows based on perennial harvest times: They sell the bulk of their late-summer-harvested perennials bareroot, shipping in the fall.

Containerizing Perennials

"We wanted to expand our selling window, so we decided to market perennials in containers," Rick says. "This opened the door to year-round sales." Goodness Grows sells perennials in gallon containers, because the "larger clumps of perennials give better results to landscapers or home gardeners," according to Rick.

Containerized perennials can also be planted any time during the year, even during periods of active growth. For southeastern customers, Goodness Grows ships perennials year-round.

Display Gardens Help Sell

"Consumer perceptions that perennials are maintenance-free and never die are delusions," Rick says. He and Marc work to dispel that myth among their retail clientele with display gardens. "The perennial garden needs annuals, bulbs, trees, shrubs—a variety of plants to add color and texture," Rick explains.

Goodness Grows is recognized locally as the first perennial business to market product through display gardens. "We assembled our first display garden to mimic a backyard setting," Rick remembers. "It went over big with our customers."

For growers who are interested in planting a display garden, Rick offers the same advice he shares with his retail customers. When choosing a location, have an astute awareness of that particular area (sun, soil, etc.); know the microclimates that are present. Rick also stresses recognizing limitations and tackling only what you can realistically manage.

New Crops Add to Perennial Assortment

Goodness Grows has introduced many perennials over the last 10 years. Rick hesitates to call them "new." Instead he says that they're "likely old plants that have ceased to be produced anymore." Where do the introductions come from? Friends, gardeners or happenstance.

- **Bath's Pink dianthus** bears single, clove-scented pink flowers on 6- to 8-inch stems. Foliage is evergreen, gray, needlelike; it takes full sun and makes a nice addition to borders or rock gardens.

- **Goodness Grows veronica** is free flowering with violet-blue flower spikes. It's been tested all over the country, from South Carolina to Pennsylvania to Texas to California and is presently being picked up by liner companies. Plant height is 18 inches; it takes full sun to partial shade.

- **Miss Huff** *Lantana camara* is a stable, hardy, substantial lantana. Flowers open yellow, then fade to orange and then pink. It's hardy as far north as Canton, Georgia, and is popular among customers in Tennessee, Alabama and North and South Carolina.

- **Oertel's Rose** *Achillea millefolium* is a dwarf (12 inches) achillea with rose-pink flowers that fade to white. Habit is spreading, and the achillea makes a good ground cover.

31

- **Abbeville *Verbena* x *hybrida*** bears large, lavender flower clusters that are fragrant. It's heat tolerant and spreads to form a ground cover. It doesn't tolerate excessive wetness. Wayside Gardens, Hodges, South Carolina, is marketing the verbena.

Along with "new" introductions, Rick also highlights two perennials that have "great potential but are underused":

- ***Rudbeckia maxima*** is an unusual yellow coneflower with 6- to 8-inch-long, bluish-silvery leaves. Flower spikes are 6 to 7 feet tall with brown cones; bloom time is late summer.

- ***Rudbeckia laciniata*** is a cut leaf coneflower that also blooms in late summer, sending up 5- to 6-foot-high, multibranched flower spikes. Flowers are a butter-yellow with green cones. Plants take shade or sun, wet or day soil.

Quick Tips from Bachman's [7]

by Julie A. Martens

Bachman's in Minneapolis, Minnesota, combines fresh and dried flowers, potted plants, a gift gallery, nursery crops and hardgoods into a floral landmark. The gift department at Bachman's offers everything imaginable for the tried-and-true gardener. From china and acrylic tableware and party items to greeting cards and toys, each item carries a floral or gardening motif. For finer collectibles, customers can select from art prints or brass, crystal or porcelain items.

The natural dried plant material is a popular department that offers a full range of services. As in the fresh flower department, customers purchase stems by the bunch—single stem or mixed—or in formal designs.

Displays Create Excitement

The "natural drieds," as Bachman's calls them, come from around the world in an array of colors. The display area reflects the natural aspect of the product, with hardwood floors, tables and latticework for displaying product.

Bachman's believes in effective display and showing people how to use the products, especially something newer like the natural drieds. It creates excitement, and suddenly, they can't keep enough of the product in stock.

As in every department at Bachman's, salespeople wrap and package the natural drieds in purple bags and give customers complete care instructions. Bachman's wants people to have good luck with their purchases.

Aquatic Plants:
an Upcoming Trend? [8]

by Russell Miller

Jim and Jan Gulley started Gulley Greenhouse, Fort Collins, Colorado, in 1975. As a wholesale and retail operation, Gulley Greenhouse has been expanding rapidly over the years to meet a rising demand in the area for annuals and perennials, due mostly to the area's changing population.

Jim and Jan have 33,760 square feet of greenhouses and 58,892 square feet of heated and unheated cold frames that are used for perennial production and hardening off plugs. They recently doubled the size of their outdoor retail display area, up to about a quarter of an acre and plan to continue increasing production space.

"We're selling more water gardens and aquatic plants. Customers are looking for more than just a lawn with grass, and water gardening is something unique that doesn't require a lot of maintenance."

The Gulleys devote as much space as they can to displaying plants in the retail greenhouse and outdoor display areas. Indoor ponds with water plants and perennial shrub displays, for example, catch customers' eyes.

"The displays help customers see how varieties look in the landscape," Jim and Jan say. "We label everything and group shrubs and perennials by color and variety so that customers can see what fall colors they can expect from each variety."

Perennials and Herbs in Demand

Perennials continue to grow in demand for Gulleys. "People are now looking for unique perennials, including smaller-sized varieties," Jan says. "They are tired of the large, common perennials. Some customers come in asking for perennials by scientific name, which shows how much more knowledgeable they are becoming.

"That's why it's important for us to educate our staff as well as our customers on the plants we have available. It's important not to concentrate totally on the new and unique, however. You also have to carry common plants, like Shasta daisies."

Plug Popper Program

Gulley Greenhouse produces about 740 varieties of perennials and is known for its Perennial Plug Popper program, sold through Ball Seed. Each year they grow 50,000 perennial and herb plug trays for wholesale and 150,000 1-gallon perennial containers for wholesale and retail. They also

FIGURE 6. *Water gardens, a growing trend, are unique, and customers like to see their possibilities displayed. Photo taken at Sperling Garden Center, Calabasas, California.*

produce 10,000 perennial flats, 10,000 annual flats, 25,000 4½-inch geraniums, 4,000 poinsettias and 150,000 3-inch herbs.

"We've been selling more herbs in the past few years. One of the reasons they are popular is that they're easy to grow," Jan says. The common herbs, like basil, are most popular, but recently the more uncommon herbs, like lemon grass, are receiving more consumer interest.

Gulley's retail herb catalog lists about 125 varieties and covers herb production, care, harvesting and preservation, and information on recipes and theme gardens. This catalog is one of three wholesale and retail catalogs they produce.

Water Gardens Are a Hit [9]

by Julie A. Martens

Hamlen's Garden Center in Swanton, Vermont, is a business with focus: They specialize in retail, landscape design and installation and effective employee management. Dave Hamlen, owner, has been in the growing business over 17 years and knows the benefits of focus.

A new niche Dave has found in the landscape area is water gardens. "Interest is definitely there and definitely increasing," he says. What's selling for Hamlen's is a 4- by 6-foot pond that can be installed for between $500 and $600.

Achieving Pond Balance

The package includes a liner with a 10-year guarantee, natural fieldstone for an informal look, plant material and fish. "We try to achieve a pond balance, planning so many oxygenating grasses, fish, snails and water lilies, per given pond size," Dave explains. The majority of the ponds are destined for private landscapes; a few go to businesses. Currently there's a 50-50 split between Hamlen- and owner-installed ponds.

The greatest challenge with ponds is educating customers that they don't have a swimming pool that will be crystal clear. Dave approaches that problem with several solutions. "We offer algicide to put into the water, but recently we're pushing an Aquashade material. It's a blue dye that colors the water so algae doesn't grow."

CHAPTER 3

Color Bowls
and Containers

---

*Extend Your Season
and Cash Flow* [1]

by Ann Turner Whitman

Increasingly, consumers are looking for convenience and instant satisfaction when they shop. They want immediate results and are willing to pay for it. How can growers and retailers cash in on this market? Preplanted color bowls and mixed containers!

Growers all over the country found it difficult to keep up with demand for color bowls and preplants last year and plan to increase production this season. Tom Wall, marketing manager, Greiling Farms Inc., Denmark, Wisconsin, reports that one of their major retail customers, a national chain store, is doubling orders for preplants for spring 1990.

The consumer buying trend in recent years has been toward larger vegetable and bedding plants—jumbo packs and 3½- to 4-inch material. Herbs and perennial have grown in popularity, too. Creative retailers and wholesalers are using these materials, as well as traditional annuals, to create preplanted containers that appeal to all segments of the market.

Containers extend selling seasons, generate repeat sales throughout the summer, and make it possible for growers to take advantage of traditionally less floral holidays. The large selection of containers also helps in creating specific themes and price categories.

Containers Make or Break Profits

Some growers offer a limited variety of pre-plant containers, use mostly traditional annuals, and design around simple themes, such as sun, shade and desert plants. Dave Grimshaw, general manager, Color Spot Foliage, Fallbrook, California, finds this approach works well for his business.

In a recent year, his company sold 124,000 14-inch color bowls, 60,000 8-inch bowls and 22,000 8- by 17-inch window boxes as preplants to chain stores and garden centers. These bowls have wide mass market appeal and are often used by the chain stores as a leader item to draw in customers.

Greiling Farms also uses mostly annuals but with a variety of containers to set the themes. Tom Wall says planter diversity broadens market appeal—cedar boxes give a country look, Grecian urns offer classic design, swan planters, bowls, strawberry jars and kettles capture mass market interest.

Tom warns, however, that "you must work hard to find containers that won't kill the cost of the item." He turns to Duraco, Arco Mills, Landmark Plastic, and Summit Plastics Co. for most of his containers, but he recommends finding a local source for wooden planter boxes to keep costs down.

Annuals Win Sales

Quality, size and variety of plants that go into the container determine its overall success in the market. Design is only limited by imagination and material on hand—seasonal plants, mixed plain and fancy annuals, herbs, perennial, dwarf shrubs, vegetables, currently popular varieties and old standbys are all useful. Preplants are a great place to introduce new varieties too limited in supply to offer as bedding packs.

Most growers recommend using large plugs and 3- to 4-inch annuals so that the preplants look "finished" after planting. These can be mixed according to color, sun/shade and moist/dry preferences, seasons and material availability. Assorted "plain" annuals, such as petunias, marigolds, salvia, pansies, alyssum, lobelia and impatiens, are used to create lower-price color bowls.

Fancy annuals—geraniums, fibrous begonias, vinca, German ivy, dusty miller and larger sizes of the common annuals—go into higher-priced preplants. Common perennials—primrose, portulaca, mums and herbs, for example, are also used. Even everbearing strawberries (in a strawberry jar, of course) are popular as container plants.

Smaller growers who sell directly to consumers often take a somewhat different approach. In addition to season extending and appeal to consumer convenience, they use preplants as an outlet for their creative talents, as a source of repeat business for the summer months, as a way to capitalize on the boom in herb and perennial sales, and as an appeal to frustrated apartment and condominium gardeners.

Keep Customers Coming Back

Duane and Monte Thompson, owners of The Greenery, a garden center in Omaha, Nebraska, use a wide variety of containers and plants to create themes. Monte, who is in charge of the designs, says that perennials and herbs are her favorites. She also designs with vegetables.

They prefer clay and wooden containers—10- to 14-inch clay pots, strawberry jars with up to 18 pockets, animal shapes and half barrels. Many barrels are sold as do-it-yourself kits that include plants and a 3-cubic foot bag of Ball mix. They always have a variety of preplants available to give customers inspiration.

Popular themes include vegetable gardens, culinary and medicinal herbs, perennial gardens, salad gardens, fragrance gardens and seasonal displays, as well as the more common annual color bowls. They view their season in three stages: extra early (March), regular (April through Memorial Day), and end of summer.

They force bulb gardens and plant them with pansies for very early sales and finish off the season with post-Labor Day pots of mums, kale, bittersweet and dwarf corn stalks.

Most preplants use a basic design format: tall plants in the middle, color and filler around the center and trailing or vining plants around the edge. Mixed leaf sizes, shapes, colors and textures create interest and enhance blooms.

Vegetable and salad gardens, popular with condo dwellers, keep customers coming back all summer for plants to replace the ones harvested. Animal-shaped pottery containers with a single herb variety and strawberry jars of mixed herbs are popular for Mother's Day. Mixed herb bowls and barrels offer tricolor sage, chives, flat and curly parsley, thyme, oregano, rue, green and opal basil, mints and others.

Scheduling and Pricing:
There's No Hard and Fast Rule

When should you start planting containers? For some, as soon as greenhouse space permits. Many producers, such as Color Spot Foliage, simply plant and send directly to retail with no grow-out time.

For this system to be successful, the plant material must be good-sized and nearly finished. They use about one 17- by 17-inch flat of material—jumbo packs and 4-inch—per 14-inch bowl. Other growers, such as Greiling Farms, utilize space left after Mother's Day sales to grow out bowls for Memorial Day, Father's Day and summer sales.

Timing also plays a role in pricing. Pre-plants are priced higher early in the season when large material, greenhouse space and labor are at a premium. Prices tend to drop after Memorial Day, but sales continue right through June and July when customers are looking for quick decorating ideas for garden parties, weddings and graduations.

Tom Wall advises, "Lawn and garden sales go all summer. It's a mistake for small retailers to get out of it early in the season." The lesson: Offer your customers variety, convenience and instant satisfaction with preplants to bring in business for extended season sales.

Theme	Container	Plant Material
Mother's and Memorial Days	7- by 15-inch planter boxes, strawberry jars, urns, kettles, baskets, animal-shaped planters	geranium, vinca, German ivy, salvia, marigold, petunia, alyssum, verbena, pansy, lobelia, impatiens, coleus, fibrous begonia, browallia, dwarf snaps, ageratum
shade	8- to 14-inch bowl	coleus, impatiens, fibrous begonia, primula
sun	8- to 14-inch bowl	marigold, alyssum, lobelia, geranium, petunia
desert	8- to 14-inch bowl	portulaca, hens and chicks, stonecrop, cactus
herb garden	strawberry jars, baskets, 15- to 16-inch pots, barrels	chives, nasturtium, green and opal basil, curly and flat parsley, oregano, orange mint, spearmint, tricolor sage, Apple Cider scented geranium, marigold, rue, lemon thyme, french thyme, garlic chives
vegetable garden	15- to 16-inch pot, barrel	trailing herbs, Sweet Chelsea tomato, Ichiban or Purple Sickle eggplant, compact sweet pepper, beets, carrots, spinach, Ruby chard, radishes, onions
salad garden	15- to 16-inch pot, barrel	leeks, scallions, parsley, carrots, radishes, mixed lettuce varieties (mix leaf colors, texture, shape), nasturtium
early spring	12- to 16-inch bowls	forced bulbs: tulip, hyacinth, grape hyacinth, daffodil, mint daffodil and pansy
perennial garden	barrel	liatris, lythrum, artemesia, miniature roses, dwarf hostas and day lilies, primula, stachys, herbs, creeping phlox, strawberries
Labor Day	8- to 9-inch bowl, barrel	mums, kale, dusty miller, bittersweet vines

Combo Planters Are Hot Sellers for the '90s [2]

by Ann Turner Whitman

Sales of combo planters have doubled in the past four years and account for an estimated 40 percent of spring plant business. Container gardens displaying mature blooming annuals and perennials not only sell themselves but also boost sales of pack and pot material, containers and tie-in merchandise. Preplanted containers sell to all levels of the market, from mass-market chain stores to upscale nurseries in affluent neighborhoods.

Appeal to customers' desires for convenience, color and ease of maintenance while giving your own late spring and summer sales a boost. Mike Mohlenhoff, Mohlenhoff's Greenhouses in Long Island, New York, says planted containers "return the highest dollar per square foot of any item displayed in the store." Here's how you can cash in on patio planters.

FIGURE 7. *Upscale terra cotta containers come in a wide range of shapes and sizes for customers to choose from. Photo taken at Mohlenhoff's Greenhouses, Long Island, New York.*

Choose Plants That Sell

Plants fall into three groups depending on their function: feature plants with an upright habit that are used in the center; trailing or edging plants that cascade over the sides; and accent plants that add balance and color. The center or feature plant should be 1½ times the height of the container for overall balance. Choose plants and containers that go well together and fit your customers' price range.

Customers are more discerning today and look for color coordination and complementary colors. Pay attention to consumer magazines and television to pick up on popular colors and themes. Hot neon colors are trendy now, as is the light, airy country look.

Geraniums Are Popular

For mass-market sales, Tom Wall, marketing manager, Greiling Farms, Denmark, Wisconsin, says they use Expeditor or 72-size annual plugs and 3½-inch geraniums in the combo planters, allowing two to six weeks grow-out time.

"Geraniums are very, very critical to our combination planter. When we plant after Mother's Day for an after-Memorial-Day finish, we start with geraniums that are cracking bud, so you can identify the color. That's our benchmark."

Mike agrees and adds, "We use only zonals in patio planters because they give a more up-scale appearance." Mike's location in an affluent Long Island neighborhood allows him to retail planters from $50 to $200. He uses 4-inch and larger material and sells the planters only 10 days after planting.

Ornamental Grasses: New for the '90s

Other popular feature plants for the up-scale market include New Guinea impatiens and perennials. "Ornamental grasses will be the hot new plants for the 1990s," says Mike. Look in nursery catalogs for the best sources. Grasses and perennials do best in 18-inch or larger containers. Nursery stock in 20-inch or larger planters appeals to affluent customers.

For edging plants, choose those with a trailing habit, such as vinca or springier fern for large planters, and compact ivy varieties, such as Glacier or Annie Gamie, for smaller pots.

Try trailing perennials such as lamiums and silver nettle vine. For blooming types, Mike likes cuphea, Mini Cascade ivy geranium, lobelia and portulaca. Accent plants include annuals, such as pansies, petunias, celosia, salvia, impatiens, marigolds and dusty miller.

Target Market, Price

When choosing containers, consider the overall effect you want to achieve, price range of the finished product, target market (upscale vs. mass-market), and logistics of handling. Plastic is the mass-market and middle-of-the-road choice because it is durable, shippable, inexpensive and available in a wide range of styles.

Cedar, redwood, terra cotta and faux stone containers appeal to the up-scale market and are also available in a wide range of sizes and styles. For hangers, consider coco-lined wire baskets.

Discover the Profit Potential in Color Bowls [3]

by Ann Turner Whitman

Make the most of your plant inventory, and extend your profits into summer with color bowls. They'll give you great marketing flexibility and help ensure strong sales throughout your plant product line. Using slow-moving, stand-alone products in bowls boosts them out the door. On the other hand, bowls also make an excellent showcase for new or popular products that may be available only in limited quantities.

According to Blair Busenbark, West Coast marketing representative for PanAmerican Seed Co., color bowls can increase profits in several ways. While they might not give you a better return on investment than packs, they do give greater access to shelf space and, therefore, greater potential for profit. Blair estimates you'd have to sell eight times more 606s than bowls at the retail level to make the same profit.

Coordinate Landscape/Patio Plantings

Trends in the premium garden center market point toward using larger bowls with space for 1-gallon material such as perennials and shrubs. To increase sales of both packs and containers, Blair suggests displaying color bowls and individual plants together to show customers how to coordinate their landscape plantings with their patio planters.

Use color bowls to help move sizes or varieties that aren't selling well. If the market for your 4-inch petunias is soft, but sales in petunia packs are strong, use the 4-inch in bowls. Blair warns against using bowls as a dump for inferior products, however. "If the product isn't good enough to sell alone," he says, "it's not good enough to put in a bowl."

Help Customers Succeed with P.O.P. Information

Most growers don't tag color bowls. Blair thinks this is a mistake because consumers have come to expect care tags on plants they buy. With high-ticket items such as color bowls, maintenance information becomes especially important. Help your customers succeed, and they'll reward you with repeat business.

Blair sees three ways to improve consumer information. The easiest method is to **use ready-made industry care tags** such as those sold by Master Tag and John Henry Company.

To tailor care information to your particular market and color bowls, Blair suggests designing pads of **tear-off information sheets** similar to those used in grocery stores for coupons and recipes.

Be sure to **use informative point-of-purchase signage** in the sales area, as well. Molbak's in Woodinville, Washington, for example, uses signs throughout its operation to help customers learn about the plants and how to use them to best advantage in and around their homes. In-store signs are best used in conjunction with tags or tear-off sheets so the customers can take the message home with them.

Stick to the Basics

Keep information on sheets, tags or signs very basic. Remind consumers to remove dead flowers and plants, to prune to keep shape and prolong bloom, to fertilize regularly with house plant fertilizer and water when dry. Additional information could include sun/shade placement and advice on how to prevent disease.

Creative Designs and Color Combinations

Too often growers simply stick a 4-inch plant in the center of a bowl and then fill the perimeter with a color pack. The result is uninspiring.

Blair thinks, "[Color bowl] designers should take a floral design course because they use the same design principles. Even visiting a florist or buying floral design magazines would be a good start."

You'll also need to understand plant heights and natural habits, as well as designing basics. Don't be afraid to design asymmetrical bowls or combine unusual colors and textures. For example, if using spike dracaena, plant it off-center.

Look for Color Trends

Color trends should also guide your choices in designing bowls. Trends start in high-priced items such as furniture and designer clothing and end in inexpensive mass-market products. When choosing design colors, look not only at the high-end color trends, but also at the color of patio and lawn furniture sold in the local department store, suggests Blair.

Try to achieve a mix in your combinations. For example, strong colors like hot rose are in fashion now, but this doesn't mean that pastels are out. Try using pastels as accents in combination with the new stronger colors. Also keep the ethnic and socioeconomic mix of your customers in mind when making color choices for bowls.

FIGURE 8. *This rosy color bowl combo is hard to beat in the heat: Salmon and White Pinwheel zinnia, Blush and Grape Cooler vinca and Easter Bonnet Violet alyssum. Photo courtesy of PanAmerican Seed Co., West Chicago, Illinois.*

Choose Foliage Plants, Too

Color bowls sell because they offer instant color. To get a jump on floral color and extend shelf-life, Blair suggests using foliage plants such as coleus or hypoestes to provide color interest, especially in bowls designed for mass marketing.

Choose plants that give long-lasting or large numbers of blooms. Torenia or *Zinnia angustifolia*, for example, are good choices for both their impressive floral displays and their relaxed texture.

Blair recommends using three to four colors per bowl. More than that makes the bowl look busy. Colors can be different shades of the same color group, such as purple, pink and lavender, or contrasting, such as red, white and blue.

Cool Classics, Warm Tones

Blue, white and cream make a cool classic. Use blue violas, ageratum, lobelia or lisianthus with white or cream-colored marigolds, Star White zinnia or shasta daisies and cream violas. Or combine warm tones, such as yellow and orange, using American marigolds with yellow petunias and thunbergia.

For a purple and yellow planter, use purple violas or petunias with yellow violas or yellow marigolds. Red and white is always a popular combination. Try red salvia with white alyssum or, for something fun and different, put Sweetheart strawberry (from seed) alone in a bowl. The plants will produce white flowers, edible, bright red fruits and glossy, dark-green foliage.

Concept Bowls: Theme Gardens in Miniature

It's not enough these days to offer just sun and shade bowls. The trend toward theme or concept gardens carries over into bowls, as well. Plant bowls with herbs or scented plants, such as Fernleaf dill, lavender, Purple Ruffles basil, or combine herbs with edible flowers for gourmet bowls using dianthus, violas and nasturtiums with parsley, chives or basil.

Plant other culinary bowls with five or six kinds of leaf lettuce or tiny cherry tomato plants. Use herbs like variegated thyme or trailing rosemary for texture and color in other floral bowls, too.

To extend your bowl-selling season into the fall or earlier into the spring, plant with cool-weather plants like pansies, viola, kale and primulas. Don't overlook the Christmas season, either. Poinsettia bowls using accent material suitable for indoor growing, such as ivy, would be good sellers.

Production Scheduling Made Simple

Grow packs and 4-inch pots for color bowls on the same schedule as if you were going to sell them separately. Use only finished plants in bowls. Blair warns against trying to grow plugs directly in the bowl because the plants will mature at different rates. He recommends planting bowls one week before shipping to allow roots to spread and to provide the best quality plants for the customer.

The most difficult part of scheduling comes long before you plant the first seed. You must plan your bowl designs and colors even before you order seeds or plugs. Thinking ahead will pay dividends, however, in increased sales and marketing flexibility.

Niche Marketing [4]

by Kim Hawks

The following original ideas by Kim Hawks are taken from *Niche Notes*, Niche Gardens' newsletter. Although written for the consumer, they offer good ideas for retailers to follow.

Create Container Niches

Specific niches that aren't available on your land can be created with containers. By using a container that doesn't drain, you can grow water lilies or bog plants. The creative use of plants completes the picture.

Herbaceous Perennials Can Work

Rather than exclusively using annuals, use them sparingly in conjunction with herbaceous perennials. Small conifers, trees and shrubs look nice in containers accompanied by a low carpet of perennial color.

Eventually these plants become too large for your containers. They can then be planted out in your yard. Or you could focus on the use of dwarf shrubs and trees to avoid future transplanting.

Soil Mix Important

A good potting mix for container plantings can be found in most garden centers. Supplement this mix with aged manure, also available in garden centers. Incorporating soil wetting agents, such as Aqua-Grow or Terra-Sorb, will increase the water holding capacity of the soil.

Finally, incorporate a slow release fertilizer (Osmocote) into the top 4 inches of soil. With all components, follow the suggested manufacturer's rates.

Make Combo Planters Your Niche [5]

by Julie A. Martens

For Michael and Mary Konkle of Konkle Farm & Greenhouses, Fenwick, Ontario, capitalizing on the instant color market has proven to be not only wise, but profitable. "I can't go head-to- head with someone with 3 to 4 acres of bedding plants who's automated," Michael admits. "We've got our niche."

Just what is that niche? Ten- to 24-inch hanging baskets and patio containers for the Toronto market and surrounding areas. It's all finished product, it's blooming, and it's selling like crazy. "With this business, we've been growing by leaps and bounds," Michael says.

Sales start in mid-April, as soon as spring breaks, and extend through mid-August. The early season sales go into Georgia and other southern states, where spring breaks while the Konkles are still shoveling snow in Ontario.

Mixed Containers and Baskets Make the Mark

The spring hanging baskets and patio containers became the mainstay at Konkle Farm & Greenhouses about four years ago. The Konkles wholesale their product to a variety of customers—from cities to garden centers to landscapers to grocery stores located from Niagara Falls to Georgia.

Typically Michael and Mary buy plugs for the specialty baskets and grow the annuals themselves. "We control our product mix and pick our own varieties," Michael explains. "We tend to go for something that's different and will perform in the landscape or streetscape."

The fiber pots arrive in early fall, and son Phillip drills holes into the pots destined for hanging baskets throughout the winter. "The finished product is big and beautiful," Mary says, "and really lets us be creative."

Plant Care Education Needed

Many of the basket- and planter-buying customers are cities or landscapers with city contracts. Mary and Michael are working hard to educate the landscapers about plant care. "If we can get our baskets out onto the streets in a city and then get them to last the summer, that translates into giving us and the town landscaper a good reputation," Michael says. "That means more sales for our garden center and grocery store customers—and ultimately more sales for us."

Although pot crops are a vital part of the crop mix, the baskets and patio planters are the mainstay, as evidenced by the collapsible benches that easily accommodate the large planters. Mary and Michael both do the growing, stressing that they don't ever want to be so large that they become "management only."

Custom Designing Containers [6]

by Russell Miller

Custom designing patio planters, hanging baskets, pots and other containers is a profitable business at McIntosh Greenhouse and Garden Center in Goshen, Indiana. Adele and Glen McIntosh started providing the service to their customers 15 years ago, about two years after they opened. Today, this service provides about 300 loyal customers with at least 600 custom-designed containers each year.

Fill 'Em Up, Please

"I'm not sure how it began," Adele says. "We had some thrifty customers who felt they should return the containers they bought rather than throw them away and buy filled ones the following year.

"We started refilling these containers with plants for our customers. The service gradually grew. Now it has become a large enough business to keep one person working full time every work day in April and May, plus an evening part-time crew of three."

When a customer brings in a container, it's tagged with the customer's name and labeled as to what should be planted in it for spring. Customers receive the same container they brought in, even if it's a common clay pot.

Always Look for the Unique

"We are always looking for unique ideas to add to the variety of custom-designed containers we do," Adele says. "We're not just filling containers with waxed begonias, for instance. We do sun-and-shade combinations, double and triple hanging gardens, and a lot of other unique plantings."

The custom-designed containers can be broken down into three groups—hanging baskets, containers up to 10 inches across, and containers up to 30 inches across—each accounting for about one-third of the total. Usually the McIntoshes start filling the containers in February or March, and customers come in to pick them up in early May.

Questions to Ask

"We have a worksheet for prices," Adele says. "Most of our customers prefer that we start the containers ourselves using our own designs. We ask questions to make sure that what we plant in each container will work for them in their setting. With impatiens, by far the largest amount of plants we use, we'll ask for certain colors the customer may want."

Gregg, company president and Glen and Adele's son, says they have some customers who bring in unusual containers to be filled, such as preformed wire birds. "We fill these with peat and soil, and then usually plug in begonias. For unusual containers or very large containers, such as those larger than 18 or 20 inches across, we'll cost out the job according to estimated time and material needed to get the job done."

Customers Take Service Seriously

"Custom designing containers is a very profitable business for us," Adele says, "and it adds dimension to our business. The customer takes this type of service seriously. It becomes a personal kind of thing. Very rarely do customers forget to come back for their custom-designed containers. I think we had only three customers this year that we had to call and remind."

Another idea they started recently and will continue in coming years is a public garden walk through the grounds where every plant variety they grow is planted and labeled.

Reserve-A-Basket [7]

by Julie A. Martens

On the Kenai Peninsula in Alaska, Trinity Greenhouse has been growing flowering plants and nursery stock for over 14 years. Dan and Ron Sexton, brothers and owners, operate 17,000 square feet of growing space in Soldotna, including a 6,120-square-foot retail area that's open from March 1 to August 1.

Hanging Baskets Are a Hallmark

The Sextons have a "Reserve-A-Basket" program that is the highlight of their retail season. "In Alaska, people are ready to put plants out in April and May, but we can get a killing frost as late as June 10," Dan says.

"We capitalize on spring fever by offering customers a chance to shop for hanging baskets—choosing from product that's in the greenhouse or from photos—starting March 1." Customers make a deposit for the baskets they want; deposits range from $15 to $25 for baskets with a 3- to 6-foot spread.

Go All the Way

Popular baskets are fuchsias, ivy geraniums and non-stop begonia and lobelia combinations. Customers pick up baskets June 1. "The reserve-a-basket system creates a lot of paperwork for us," Dan admits, "but it's all part of customer service. The customer is truly king in our greenhouse. For the small grower, especially in retail, you've got to go all the way to meet customer demands."

Above All, Be Different [8]

by Neal Catapano

Bedding plant retailing in America still continues to change—and change rapidly, says Neal Catapano, Catapano Farms, Southold, Long Island, New York. The most interesting and far-reaching changes have been made in the last decade. Not only have bedding plant sales risen dramatically, but new marketing channels—department stores, hardware stores, discounters and warehouse outlets—have drastically increased consumer exposure to plants.

FIGURE 9. *Color bowls are finished, blooming products with wide appeal that can extend your selling season. Photo taken at PanAmerican Seed pack trials, West Chicago, Illinois.*

Competition is getting tougher. Wholesale suppliers are shipping better quality, and the stores are taking better care of plants. Also, prices are starting to come down. The bedding plant grower-retailer, however, does have a number of unique advantages that he can use to compete success-fully with mass merchandisers.

Be Unique

Mass merchandisers would love to turn flowers into a commodity item, the living equivalent of soap or toothpaste. And there's only one way to compete on a commodity item: price. The bedding plant grower-retailer must fight any attempt of mass merchandisers to impress upon the public's mind that "plants is plants." At every opportunity, present your plants as something different from the ordinary.

Figure out what type of flat the competition is using, and physically grow your plants in something radically different. If your market is saturated with cookie cutter 1204s, switch to a Connecticut or California flat. Or try 804s or even 1603s. Or environmentally friendly Jiffy strips. It's important to have a look that's completely different from the mass merchandiser down the street.

CHAPTER 4

Employee Management

You Can Become a Better Employee Manager [1]

by Steven and Suz Trusty

Finding and keeping good personnel is tough. People problems are much the same, whether you run a family operation with a few non-family employees or a large corporation with multiple management levels and hundreds of employees. Managers tend to assume that everyone knows certain things about the company and their place in its operation. Often this is far from true.

Employee surveys over the last decade repeatedly report what management has been complaining about—even by their own ratings, most employees don't give 100 percent on the job.

Why?

Managers say employees want more money and more job security. Employees say they want more appreciation and more input on what is going on. The most repeated reason given by employees for not putting out 100 percent is: "I don't know how my efforts contribute to the organization's success."

If your employees don't think what they do really matters, what difference does it make how well they do it? Yet, front line workers have the most frequent contact with your customers.

Circulate Your Business Philosophy

- What is your business philosophy? Why are you in business? What do you want to accomplish? Where do you want to be 10 years from now or 20 years from now? How do you want your customers to talk about your business? Even an individual, running a business on his own, needs to know this. If you don't know where you are going, how will you ever get there?

- Write it down. Read it out loud. Does it say what you feel and believe? When it does, let everyone in your company know about it. If your employees don't know why the business was established and what it is meant to accomplish, how can they possibly help make it happen?

Write Down Job Descriptions

- Do you have written job descriptions for everyone in the company? You say, "There are only six of us, and everybody knows what he's supposed to do." Are you sure?

  Remember when XYZ Garden Center didn't get called about the changed delivery schedule? How about the problem in the greenhouse watering system? Who was supposed to check it out? Who didn't follow-up with that customer whose bill is now 90 days past due?

Skills Checklist

How are your skills in employee management? Check them out by answering these ten questions.

1. Do you have a set business philosophy that is known and can be repeated by your employees?
2. Have you given each employee at your business a written job description?
3. Have you told each employee how his work contributes to the business's success?
4. Do you establish work priorities—and stick to them?
5. Do you hold regular company meetings to keep everyone up to date?
6. During the past two weeks, have you asked an employee, "How's it going?"— and really listened to the answer?
7. During the past two weeks, have you told an employee he had done a good job?
8. Do you let your employees finish a sentence?
9. Do you stay back and let an employee tackle a task?
10. Do you react calmly to an employee error?

Three or more "no" answers and you may want to take another look at how you are working with employees. Learn how to help employee managers become people managers.

- Put in writing the basic tasks to be completed by each employee—yourself included. You may discover that Joe never gets his work done because he has too many things to do. Or that Peggy could handle a fourth of Joe's work along with her own and still have time to spare. The business may have more to do than people to do it, or too many people for what needs doing.

  There will be times when Joe will have to help Peggy, and you will have to help them both. That's great—you'll all be working together to accomplish the goals of the business. Peggy will know that she can call on Joe in a pinch and will be far more willing to help him when he needs it.

  Since all important tasks are the responsibility of some person, you will be more confident that these tasks are being completed or that you will be aware of problems before they reach the disaster stage.

- Some tasks, such as serve the customer, will appear on everyone's list. If customer service is a major part of your business philosophy, it should be on everyone's list.

  What does this really mean? No matter what else your people are doing, they will concentrate their efforts on making sure that your customers receive the kind of treatment they should. Could anything be more important than that?

Explain Employee Tasks

- Does each employee know how his work contributes to the business as a whole? You have let every employee know what the business is there for and what their specific tasks are. Now put the pieces together.

  Let Peggy know that every time she answers the phone she is the business's link to that customer. She has the responsibility to let each person she talks to know that the company is glad they called, even if they called to complain. Her actions toward every customer who calls shape that customer's image of the entire company.

  Joe needs to know that every time he carries a tray of flats to the customer's car, he is the last contact the entire company will have with that customer. A friendly smile, cheerful conversation and careful handling of the plants will go a long way toward bettering the customer's impression of the company.

- Explain how each task on each employee's list contributes to the operation of the business. Tasks repeated daily become easier to perform well when people know how and why they matter.

Keep Company Goals in Mind

- Do you establish work priorities and stick to them? No one likes to put out effort that is wasted. If you consistently change the plan of action for the day and pull an employee off one project to start on another, that employee is going to have problems finishing a job.

  Everyone encounters emergencies at the company that require a quick shift of plans. The problem arises when every day is an emergency.

- Try keeping a weekly and daily "TO DO" lists. Check the assignments given to each employee to see how frequently they are done on the day assigned. If they are not being completed then, dig into why this is happening.

  You may discover an ineffective or overworked employee or that your long-range planning tends to be more like "seat of the pants." Keep the company goals in mind, and make sure all projects will eventually contribute to those company goals.

Keep Employees Informed

Do you hold regular meetings to keep everyone up to date? Sure, you're too busy, and it's next to impossible to get everyone together at one time in one place. That's exactly why these meetings are so important.

Your employees are a team working together for the good of the company. Can you imagine a football team going into the huddle and excluding the quarterback and wide receiver or the right tackle? Obviously, whatever play was called would fall apart.

That's just what happens within your business when you attempt to carry out plans without alerting all the employees. Are you having a Saturday open house, advertising a big special, or converting a production house to display? Every employee should know about it, why it's happening, and how they can help make it a success.

Company meetings can be as informal as a half-hour jam session over coffee and doughnuts before opening. Get everyone together and do it.

Show Interest in Employees

Have you asked "How's it going?" and really listened to the answer? People are not machines. They have bodies. They have minds. They have feelings. They have a whole network of other people with whom they interact.

Some days they are just not going to feel good. They may have a lousy cold, a sick child or trouble with their cars. Some days they are going to feel super. They've just passed a physical with flying colors, their kid got straight A's on the last report card, and they can finally afford to get the car fixed.

What happens to them does concern you. All these factors have an impact on their performances at work. You don't need to become a counselor for all your employees. You don't have an obligation to solve all their problems. But you do need to acknowledge that they are human, and show an interest in their lives. Even the bad days are easier to work through if someone just shows a bit of interest.

Praise Employees

- Have you told an employee that he's done, or is doing, a good job? Everyone likes to hear a little praise now and then. But the praise must be genuine. Keep your eyes open for superior performance, and let the employee know you appreciate it. Tell him in front of others.

- If you see problems in employee performance, let them know that, too, but not at the same time. Don't combine praise and complaint. If you always start with the good and head into the bad, the employee will just be waiting for the real reason for the conversation, the bad news.

- Never reprimand anyone in front of others. Express the problem to the individual one to one. Be sure he understands your complaint. Agree on the proper action to be taken. Then be quiet about it. Watch to make sure the problem is being resolved, but don't be obvious about it. Assume the best unless you are shown otherwise.

Listen to Employees

- Do you let your employees finish a sentence? Before answering yes to this one, think about it for a couple days as you go through the work day. Surprised? Most managers are.

  During the hectic everyday schedule such common courtesy seems to fall by the wayside. Managers assume that they already know what was going to be said and act on that assumption.

  How do employees feel about it? Frustrated, sometimes angry; many report just giving up trying to communicate with the boss. "If he already thinks he knows all the answers, why should I bother to fill him in? If it's bad news, he'll probably just gripe about it anyway. Let him find out for himself."

- Try closing your mouth until the other person has finished speaking. Initially, you might even have to clamp your teeth together to keep from jumping in. (This may be especially true with family members working together.) Try it for one week. You'll be so pleased with the results, it'll become a habit.

57

Properly Train Employees

- Do you stay back and let an employee tackle a task? Again, this is harder to do in practice than it appears. You've probably done the same job yourself a thousand times, you know just what needs to be done, and you can probably do it better and faster. And you always will, if you don't give the employee the opportunity to develop.

  Have you ever taught a child to ride a bike? Remember all that running up and down the sidewalk holding up the bike and thinking he'd never get the hang of it? How does he ride now? Give your employees the training they need to perform their assigned tasks. Then get out of the way, and let them at it.

Don't Let Mistakes Happen Twice

- Do you react calmly to an employee error? If your employees are not making mistakes, they are probably not doing much. Mistakes are an integral part of the learning process.

  Granted, some of this learning is expensive. Plants are damaged; equipment is mistreated; orders are mixed up. Are you really paying people to make such a mess of things? No, you're paying for on-the-job training.

- Your method of handling such errors determines how effective this training will be. Don't attempt to gloss over the mistakes. Talk about them calmly with the employee. Point out the problems that occurred and how they can be avoided in the future.

  Try to find out what contributed to the mistake. Is a demonstration of proper procedures sufficient, or will the employee need additional technical training? Take the necessary steps to avoid the same mistake in the future.

- Good training means employees won't make the same mistake twice. It is usually beneficial to retain an otherwise good employee who has made an expensive error. You've already invested that much in bringing him to this point, why throw that training away?

  When you handle employee mistakes fairly, employees will be more likely to approach you at the early stages of such problems when there is a far greater opportunity to correct things before too much damage occurs.

- Does all this sound like a lot of work? Did anyone ever tell you good management was an easy job? But the rewards to you in terms of personal satisfaction and to the business in more effective and more profitable operation make it all worthwhile.

---

14 Ways to Get and Keep Good Employees [2]

by Russell Miller

The No. 1 aspect about garden center retailing is the people we work with—our employees. With this approach, Bob Maddux, owner of Delhi Flower and Garden Centers in Cincinnati, Ohio, has developed a method of employer-employee relationships he calls *The Delhi Way.*

Bob has more than 60 full-time employees working for him during the peak spring bedding plant production months in two, 60,000-square-foot garden centers and 20,000 square feet of wholesale production greenhouses. Bob says his employee turnover rate is probably much lower than the average garden center's turnover rate, simply because of *The Delhi Way.*

"There is a crisis in the retail segment of this industry," he says. "I think the No. 1 problem we have is the shortage of good garden center employees. The second problem is service."

Employers and Employees Work Together

Employers must think of their employees as "partners," Bob adds. "I wouldn't be here today without the good, key employees I now have.

"The best way for small retailers to compete with the big guys is with employees. Our employees must be able to offer service. In other types of retail stores, when you walk through any retail area, the employee doesn't even look you in the face. Garden center employees should greet customers and provide service. That's the key to successful retailing."

Since the first Delhi Flower and Garden Center opened about 30 years ago, Bob has been working on perfecting *The Delhi Way* . Here are Bob's 14 points of *The Delhi Way* and his reasoning behind the concepts.

1. It's the grower's role to train employees.

"We have to work harder with vocational training programs in high schools. Growers should work with high school vocational programs during school months. Then offer the students in those programs a summer job; offer them training."

2. Recruit only good employees.

"When we interview prospective employees, we give a written test that is available from a national agency. This test helps determine if that employee has a problem with drugs, alcohol or honesty. We usually only hire the ones who completely pass this test. It's important, however, to consider every prospect individually."

3. Offer perks to keep employees.

"My objective is to recruit employees who will either stay with Delhi or stay in the industry. Some of Delhi's best part-time employees are now going to college. We are looking into providing scholarships for employees who want to go to college, but can't afford it. The idea is to give the employee an education, then get that employee back after graduating. You should offer anything you can to keep or get a good garden center employee."

4. Encourage enrollment in the right college courses.

"You don't need a college degree in horticulture to water plants. Besides horticulture-related courses, students should take business courses so that they understand all aspects of business. That's the kind of education they need to run a successful garden center."

5. Pay employees well, and make them happy.

"Pay employees by responsibilities, not just by experience. Give employees decent tools to work with and decent facilities to work in. If you have good people, make life easier for them at work. Isn't that what owners want—to make their own lives easier? That's what employees do for the owner, so return the favor."

6. Get to know your employees.

"I try to remember the first name of every employee who works for me. When I see that person, I'll call him or her by name, and if time permits, we talk with each other. I make an effort to learn more about an employee's life outside of work. Employees really appreciate it when you can remember names and talk about their hobbies or future goals in life."

7. Allow for suggestions.

"We put up a suggestion box for employees. These suggestions go straight to me and not through anyone else—that's very important.

"One employee suggested we create a lunch room since they were eating lunches in the greenhouse. So we put in a lunchroom with nice tables and chairs. It made an obvious difference to the employees.

"Another employee suggested we lower the vent chains so that she could reach them without having to get a chair. We did, and she now knows that we care about her. These kinds of things may cost a little money, but to the employees, the rewards can be better than a raise."

8. Buy employees lunch, throw a party or a picnic.

"Spring for lunch on a very busy day or after a very busy week. Your employees work very hard for you to get the job done on time. Buying them a nice lunch and allowing them the time to enjoy it at work is well worth the price of the meal.

"We put on a summer picnic and a Christmas party, which may cost us $5,000, but it's well worth it. Get your employees involved with other employees, not just at work but after work, too."

9. Show recognition.

"We give recognition plaques to all our three-year and five-year employees, usually during our picnics and parties. Even part-time employees get plaques. I hand the plaques out directly to the recipient, and that's important. Every five years thereafter, we give out another plaque.

"We all get better as time goes by. Give little praises but not phony praises. Compliment employees when they treat a customer with a problem the right way or when the benches look especially nice. Even the worker at the lowest level deserves and respects compliments."

10. Keep criticism constructive.

"Don't jump all over a worker if something is wrong, and never criticize an employee while others are present. Take that employee into an office, and speak in a normal tone of voice. Tell the employee what's wrong and how to improve. Sometimes the fault may lie with the teacher's instructions not with the student's ability to do the job. Criticism should be short and to the point, but most of all, it should be constructive."

11. Put employees in charge.

"Our productivity has gone up since I started putting other people in charge of running a department or being responsible for part of the work. It's hard for an owner to allow others to do the important jobs, but it's one of the best ways to increase productivity."

12. Arrange planning sessions.

"Once I pushed our growers to grow more plants. Then I noticed that quality was going down. We had a meeting, and I realized that by pushing for quantity, the growers were forced to sacrifice quality because we didn't have the necessary bench space. Now we have planning sessions before every growing season. This way, the growers can tell me what they can and can't grow with the facilities and abilities we have."

13. Expect high results.

"Don't settle for second-rate work. You expect a lot from yourself, so expect a lot from your employees. If a worker doesn't produce, replace the worker. As an owner, you'll be replaced if you don't produce."

14. The ex-employee is important.

"Sometimes you'll hire a worker and then realize that person is the wrong person for your business. If the employee decides to quit, say 'goodbye' and 'good luck.' Also say, 'I hope you come back if you change your mind in the future.'

"Some young employees need time to mature. We have employees who left and when they came back, say, from college four years later, we rehired them. They worked out fine the second time around."

How to Avoid Mutiny in the Greenhouse [3]

by Dave Hamlen

Remember the story of *Mutiny on the Bounty*, when the ship's crew rose up against Captain Bligh? In the greenhouse business, our *Bounty* is the "loot" we earn during the business year.

How do employees perceive this? Do they see it as something of which they have very little while the boss has it all? Do they feel we're lining our pockets while handing them a meager ration?

A Swiss Bank Account?

My retail business had a part-time employee who operated the cash register during spring rush. This employee was positive we had a Swiss bank account. Telling this person we worked long hours and actually received a fraction of the money collected did little good. Other employees shared the same opinion.

Employees communicate extremely well with one another when one feels conditions are unfair. A mutiny? Well, perhaps not. But to say all our employees were content wouldn't be correct either.

In talking with other business owners I've learned that employees are usually complaining about something. They feel they're tools to get the business or owners where they want to be. If they're not useful, then they're expendable.

In Captain Bligh's day these "expendable" people would be sentenced to walk the plank. If you must let an employee go, just be aware of your state's laws regarding employee termination. Perhaps you can modify some of your attitudes or policies instead to improve employee performance.

Disclose, Motivate, Communicate, Recognize

If an employer has a poor attitude toward employees, it's no wonder they're contemplating mutiny. Business owners needn't worry; they'll not be put off their own ship. But they may not see their ship proceeding on the course they would like, or—worse yet—they may see the ship slowly sinking because of employees' careless attitudes.

Not wanting a mutiny or disgruntled workers, I felt we needed to get our garden center "ship" on course. To do this we implemented these changes:

- **Show financial statements or monthly balance sheets to all employees.** Now, for the first time, employees could see where the gravy was going. We didn't hear any more about Swiss bank accounts. Not only did employees see the business's financial workings, but they felt a more integral part of the business now that they were privy to this financial information.

- **Let employees assume responsibility.** When an employee realizes he's responsible for making his department profitable, his job takes on new meaning. Increase that awareness by providing a bonus or profit-sharing program, so employees are working with you and not for you.

- **Communicate more with employees.** Let people know what's happening in the business. We now inform them why deliveries are late, why customers complain, or how customers appreciate our products or services.

- **Put key employees through a personal self-improvement course.** This has helped our employees communicate better with customers. When employees relate to customers, then customers can relate to your business.

- **Recognize employees.** Recognizing employees is one of the best ways to keep people happy. Appreciation will cause an employee to try harder. Recognition can be in the form of a gift certificate, food, entertainment or even a smile and handshake.

  I've been keeping an appreciation calendar. On the calendar I put down the employee's name, the date I showed appreciation and what for. This is one way I document my recognition. It also shows me which employee seems to be trying harder or who is receiving the greatest amount of appreciation.

- **Employee trips.** Another way to keep employees happy is to take them on trips. Taking employees to trade shows, meetings or to visit other greenhouses creates enthusiasm for your business. Employees feel like they're more a part of the business.

  If you show employees what's expected of them to meet financial obligations, if you communicate with them, give them responsibility and help educate them, then they'll help take your ship wherever you want to go. Your business will start to look less like a meeting and more like the paradise Captain Bligh's men found in Tahiti!

Getting the Most From Your No. 1 Resource—Employees [4]

by John H. Saxtan

Good employees are your business's most important resource, and finding, hiring and keeping good employees is one of the most important aspects of a manager's job. You probably have some good employees you wish you could clone, but that isn't possible.

What is possible was the subject of a seminar presented at *GrowerExpo '89* by Robal Johnson, formerly of RAJ Associates, a Chicago consulting firm. You can learn some basic techniques that will help you find and keep employees who are worth their weight in gold.

Finding and Keeping Employees

In some parts of the country, finding good employees may be as hard as keeping them. Robal recommends both conventional and not-so-conventional means for finding good employees.

If your employment market is tight, **run a help wanted ad** describing the job as attractively as possible, but beware of giving too much information away. If you use words such as "aggressive self-starter wanted," or "a good job for a person with high energy," you are telling interviewees how they should act when you talk to them. Avoid behavioral descriptions such as "hard working," "energetic" and "friendly" in ads.

Referrals from current employees are another resource. Robal suggests a "finder's fee" be paid to the employee who helps find a new employee, but that the fee be split into two parts. The first part is paid when the recommended person is hired, the second half after the person has been employed six months or so. "This helps your cash flow and minimizes any chance of funny business," he says.

A third method of finding good employees is an idea Robal calls **PBWA (Prospecting By Walking Around).** In short, it's stealing good employees from another employer. "But that's ok," says Robal, "if it's done discreetly. Chances are that most people you hire will already be working for someone else, so you're always stealing from another employer." When you have defined behaviorism and skills you want in an employee, go to places where people with those skills are working.

If you need a retail sales person, visit retail stores. When you see someone who deals with people the way you want them to, approach that person, compliment them and ask them to call you if they have any prospects in mind. The advantage here is that you can observe a person working, not just how they say they work.

Asking the Right Questions

If you run an ad and expect to get a lot of responses, run a "blind" ad without your name and address. "This eliminates your need to respond to each one or to keep records—just throw away the ones that don't interest you."

If you expect to receive fewer responses, or if your company has a special appeal, by all means run your name and address, but be prepared to respond. One way to control this is to run only a phone number. A 10- or 15-minute phone interview can help narrow the list to those you seriously want to interview.

When interviewing, use open-ended questions that call for a decision on the interviewee's part. Instead of "Did you enjoy college?" ask "What did you like best about college?" The responses will tell you a lot about a person, what is important to them, and how they might fit into your company.

If you say, "Tell me about yourself," and the person fumbles around and doesn't know quite what to say, chances are that person may not be a good decision maker. Listen carefully to the content and the behavior revealed. Does the person ramble on, or does he or she highlight key points that relate to your business or how the person might work out as an employee?

Gut reaction plays an important role in deciding who to hire. "Always trust your gut reaction when it's negative," says Robal, "but never trust it when it's positive." An overly positive impression can create a "halo" that may make you overlook shortcomings, so keep interviewing. If you remain positive about that person, fine, but give your other senses a chance to react.

It's a Matter of Motivation

Once you've hired good employees, how do you keep them from being lured away? Robal says that many managers fail to recognize that their job "is to help the people who work for them be successful."

How do you encourage success? Praise employees when they do a job well, and they will try to do it better next time—even when you aren't around. "Feedback is the breakfast of champions," Robal says. "It should be given regularly and in large doses."

Recognition and praise are keys to motivating your employees. Give employees more responsibilities, and they feel more important. Listen to your employees, both to hear what they have to say and to let them know that you care about them.

If you search out good prospects, listen to their behavior when you interview them, and motivate with praise and recognition once you hire them, you can get the most from your most important resource: your employees.

Making Family Business Work—Beyond Bloodlines [5]

by Julie A. Martens

For Chris Conant, taking over the business at Claussen's Florist & Greenhouse, Colchester, Vermont, meant stepping in as the first non-family owner in the company's long history. The transition from employee to owner was a difficult one—not only for Chris, but also for the 35 full-time, year-round people who are employed at Claussen's.

Walking a Management Tightrope

When Chris first took over, managing the employees presented a tough challenge. Imagine having worked with a group of people for three years—just out of college—and then being made their boss.

Chris had no formal management training, but he began with an attitude that focused on treating all employees equally and stating frequently that he couldn't do the job alone. The Claussen's management team comprises retail managers at the four stores, a full-time grower living on-site in Colchester, a physical plant manager, a propagator, a bookkeeper/office manager (Chris's wife) and two wholesale sales reps.

"When I took over, I had sufficient staff with experience, so I let them do their jobs and concentrated on developing a long-range business plan," Chris explains. "That let them know I trusted them and that I intended to keep the business running—for a long time."

Chris's Golden Rules

When asked about his Golden Rules of employee management, Chris responds without hesitation. "You've got to be willing to work with people—loading the trucks, filling pots, whatever. I make it a point to spend time with each person daily."

Next on Chris's list is addressing employees' problems as if they were his own. "I realize that everyone here has the same financial and personal problems as I do. I just deal with each one individually."

Equal Treatment Builds Confidence

Letting people prove themselves is another top priority for Chris. "I treat everyone equally, and I can honestly say that I rarely lose my temper. That gives people the confidence to try things they might not otherwise."

Investing time in the industry's future is one part of Chris's management philosophy that is "especially rewarding." Claussen's works with local vo-tech centers, hiring two students in the spring and fall. "I spend extra time with these students, encouraging them. Who knows? This may become their occupation." So far, Claussen's has hired one of these vo-tech students who pursued a horticulture degree.

Other Benefits

In addition to his own brand of management, Chris provides weekly smoking prevention programs and paid vacation and medical benefits. He also avoids liquid chemical applications in the interest of employee safety.

"My key issue is maintaining a healthy employee relationship," Chris emphasizes. "Service to them is just as important as to my customers."

Management—the Key to Molbak's Future [6]

by Russell Miller

With 160 employees during the peak spring production months and a base staff of 120, management plays an important role at Molbak's Greenhouse, Woodinville, Washington. Each department in the business—the nursery, garden center, gift shops and wholesale and retail greenhouses—has managers. Jerry Wilmot, who was the general manager then, explains Molbak's philosophy.

"We're striving for the best possible customer service and a well-educated staff. Our prevailing management objective is to treat our employees with a lot of respect, because they are the people who work with our customers the most. Our goal is to improve each year," Jerry says.

High Efficiency and Quality

"We also have to become more efficient while producing the wide variety of plants we need for retail," Jerry says. "We have to ensure that wholesale and retail quality stays high while we remain competitive on our prices."

"Our future is in the same direction that we have followed in the past," owner Egon Molbak adds. "We strive for excellence. We want to provide the best for our employees and our customers—both wholesale and retail."

Employee Development [7]

by Julie A. Martens

"Happy and successful gardening." That's the closing Steve Elliott, manager at Elliott's Greenhouses & Garden Centers in Vermont, uses in his seasonal greeting to customers on the front page of the company newsletter. It's also been the theme behind over 26 years of successful business, highlighted by increasing sales, conscientious employee development, and innovative crop production.

Elliott's combines wholesale and retail sales at a growing/retail location located in Lyndon Center, Vermont, and a second retail site in Stowe. Customers and commercial accounts come from within a 75-mile radius.

Expansion Comes to a Standstill

1990 was the first year in company history that greenhouse construction didn't occur; 1991 was the second. Steve explains, "These last two years I've stopped expanding and started devoting more time to employee development."

The staff at Elliott's includes six full-time, plus 26 full-time seasonal workers. With business divided dollar-volume-wise 50-50 between retail and wholesale, Steve finds it challenging to hire skilled people who can handle the product and service diversity.

Emphasis on Education, Development

"I've been putting tremendous effort this year into educating and developing the staff in sales and growing. We've toured garden centers to generate retail display ideas and visited perennial gardens to enhance our design and variety offerings," he says.

One-third of the seasonal full-time staff returned from 1990 to 1991, and Steve anticipated the figure would jump to 50 percent for 1992. Why the high return rate? "I've been fortunate to find people who are talented and interested in their jobs." Health insurance and bonuses are also drawing cards for employees.

Everyone receives a percentage of the bonus, based on three criteria: meeting sales goals, customer satisfaction with landscape projects, and co-worker evaluations. Co-workers score each other's productivity and teamwork on a scale of 1 to 5.

Training Builds Business [8]

by Russell Miller

Campbell's Nurseries and Garden Centers, founded in 1912 by Bob Campbell's father, has two retail outlets: the original 9-acre garden center and gift shop near midcity Lincoln, Nebraska, and a southside 125-acre nursery and commercial landscaping department. Recently, a 21-acre retail branch opened on the northeast side of Lincoln.

"We have planned meetings on salesmanship for the employees," Bob says, "but I'm thinking about taking it a step further by doing some videotapes on customer service for new employees—like how to answer the phone, make a sale, give advice and answer customers' questions.

"I've always believed that this business is successful for three reasons: Our employees are so pleasant that people like to shop here, we have knowledgeable people working here, and we have quality products. These are things that will keep this business as successful as it has been in the past.

"This business isn't built on one person; it isn't me, it isn't Dick, Doug, Mike or Sandy. It's built on the good people we surround ourselves with, the people working at Campbell's."

CHAPTER 5

Customer Service

Make Serving Customers Your Organization's Driving Force [1]

by Ivan C. Smith

Customer satisfaction is the foundation for both a business's growth and its financial well being. Management commitment is the first requirement in responding to customer needs at every level of the organization. This includes not just the company's president but the entire management team.

At The Color Yard, a Houston, Texas, floral wholesaler and retailer, Chris Brooks, president, leads the way. She says, "A customer's criticism of our operation is a compliment because it shows that the customer cares enough to share his or her concerns with us." Three Color Yard buyers maintain direct and regular contact with wholesale customers, encouraging them to specify their product and service needs.

APIE Customer Response

The Color Yard makes use of an effective technique called APIE—for Assessment, Planning, Implementation and Evaluation—in responding to customer concerns.

In the **Assessment** phase of APIE, a group of employees involved with a particular issue studies current practices, identifying resulting successes and failures. Next comes **Planning**.

Here the group identifies possible strategies for correcting an unsatisfactory situation. Employees then select specific strategies, which they put into practice during the subsequent **Implementation** phase.

The **Evaluation** step involves assessing the effectiveness—through customers' eyes—of the implemented strategies, continuing the never-ending process of measuring customer satisfaction performance.

Chris Brooks describes the use of APIE in solving a customer problem: The Color Yard identified, through assessment of customer information collected in regularly scheduled surveys, the annoying phenomenon of telephone customers being on "hold" for extended periods.

The Color Yard's job description excerpts show customer satisfaction components.

Wholesale manager job description
Priority No. 1: Maintain quality customer service

A) Keep high profile with current customers, either in person or by phone.

B) Phone most active customers weekly to verify their needs, upcoming bids and bookings for future orders.

C) Survey active customers to assess plant quality, service.

Color buyer/wholesale sales job description
Priority No. 1: As a member of The Color Yard team, I feel customer service is No. 1. If we have happy customers, we increase sales, which increases profits. My objectives in this area include:

A) Greet customers as soon as possible.

B) Answer calls promptly.

C) Know contractors and their preferences.

D) Set up deliveries and help them go smoothly.

E) Help customer find alternatives for out-of-stock plants, special order such plants and call customer as soon as they arrive.

F) Use my knowledge to answer questions, give suggestions and diagnose problems.

G) Invoice promptly and coordinate loading either by doing it myself or finding other employees to help.

H) Work with customers to correct any problems that arise so that they'll be happy.

I) Stay in touch with customers through industry meetings, yard parties, seminars, conventions and conversation in the wholesale office.

A Team Solution

The Color Yard assembled a team to deal with the issue, a routine approach for the firm, which practices team management as a way of business life. The planning team identified two possible approaches for dealing with the problem. One was to dedicate a separate telephone operator to handle wholesaler calls. The other was for the telephone operator to routinely implement two paging routes—an internal one through the telephone system and an external one through speakers located throughout The Color Yard's 4.6-acre facility.

The team opted for the dual paging system. It now has been in effect for a short time. The target is for no caller to experience more than 30 seconds on hold. Now all Color Yard employees are expected to respond to calls on hold.

If the call is for Joe, for example, and Mary sees that Joe is busy working with another customer, she'll pick up the telephone, apologize for the delay, and either offer to help the caller herself or have Joe return the call later.

Customer Satisfaction Comes First

All Color Yard team members focus constantly on their individual roles in customer satisfaction as well as their customer satisfaction team roles. In regular training sessions they study and discuss video tapes highlighting effective customer service practices.

Management team members work closely with individual Color Yard employees, counseling them in ways to assist all customers whose needs vary from wanting lots of attention to preferring to be left alone until they have a question.

All Employees Serve All Customers

All Color Yard employees are constantly alert for the customer—whether retail or wholesale—who needs help, and when they spot a need, they immediately jump in and fill it. Indeed, ability to be a team player is a prerequisite for employment at The Color Yard.

Customer satisfaction responsibilities are an important part of The Color Yard's job descriptions. Naturally, customer satisfaction performance is a major topic discussed during performance appraisals.

The Color Yard conducts regular employee meetings. Management meets every Thursday and the entire organization one Thursday a month. In addition, retail employees meet every Sunday. A key agenda item at these meetings is reporting progress in achieving customer satisfaction goals.

Management meetings include non-managerial employees, who have unusually high customer contact levels, a device for keeping management attention focused on customer satisfaction.

Surveys Guide Solutions

Soon, The Color Yard will conduct another quarterly customer satisfaction survey. During that survey, the effectiveness of the new telephone paging system will be assessed and changed, if necessary. Customer survey findings will guide the decision.

Chris Brooks isn't satisfied that The Color Yard has established an adequate linkage between customer satisfaction and compensation. She reports definite progress in this direction, however. For one thing, there's the fact that customer satisfaction responsibilities have been identified in job descriptions.

Furthermore, in keeping with The Color Yard's management philosophy of open communications, the firm has recently begun sharing key financial data with all employees. So the stage has been set for establishing the desired linkage.

How-to Clinics Please Customers

One key outcome of The Color Yard's customer focus is providing the organization with a tremendous competitive advantage: The company regularly conducts "how-to" clinics for both its retail and wholesale customers.

Topics covered in the clinics are those suggested by the customers themselves during surveys. Customers frequently report that no other supplier conducts such clinics: Several have cited the clinics as a major reason for their buying from The Color Yard.

How does The Color Yard's dedication to customer satisfaction affect its business? Chris and others at The Color Yard know they're outperforming competition in this vital area because customers tell them so.

Viewed in absolute terms, is The Color Yard's customer service merely good or is it excellent? Reflecting one of her fundamental management beliefs, Chris says, "How about 'Good Plus?' There's always room for improvement!"

Company principles vital to enhancing customer satisfaction

1. Top management commitment
2. Listening to customer concerns
3. Analysis of customer concerns
4. Responsiveness to customer concerns
5. Understanding individual employee's customer satisfaction roles
6. Understanding team employee's customer satisfaction roles
7. Linking customer satisfaction with job descriptions and performance appraisals
8. Linking customer satsifaction with compensation and recognition practices
9. Continuous measuring of customer needs and success in satisfying those needs

©1993, by Ivan Campbell Smith Inc.

Use Surveys to Define and Measure Retail Customer Satisfaction [2]

by Ivan C. Smith

Customer satisfaction isn't some extra consideration in a business. Rather, it's the very reason for a company's existence. Providing a higher level of customer satisfaction than competitors do is the single most important strategic challenge facing an organization.

Customer satisfaction is probably the No. 1 determinant of continued profitability. In any competitive situation, the one who does the best job satisfying customers is likely to enjoy the greatest market share and the highest prices.

It's not the exclusive responsibility of people in the marketing division to worry about customer satisfaction. Rather, it's the responsibility of all employees. Having satisfied customers requires that all the people in a company work together in a cooperative and coordinated manner.

Given the importance and the nature of customer satisfaction, it follows that representatives from the entire organization should be involved in the customer satisfaction effort, including the definition and measurement process. Your best bet is to establish a task force for defining and measuring customer satisfaction.

Ask Customers to Define Satisfaction

The first step in achieving outstanding customer satisfaction is to define just what it is. The next step is to measure the company's performance in providing it.

As the task force begins to define customer satisfaction, it's vital they don't assume they already know what supplier attributes customers consider most important. That's a mistake, believe it or not, that occurs frequently.

A key point to remember in defining customer satisfaction is to use the customers' definition, not your own. To learn what supplier attributes customers consider important, of course, you have to ask them.

Include the Customers Who Buy and Those Who Don't

Your best approach for defining and measuring customer satisfaction among retail customers is to conduct intercept interviews as customers leave your store. This way, you'll learn their views immediately while they're still fresh in the customers' minds.

Be sure to include both those customers who have made purchases and those who haven't. The latter group—though in some cases more challenging to interview—will provide you with very valuable information on how you might develop your business.

Constructing an Intercept Interview

The interview will take from seven to 12 minutes, unless a respondent is especially eager to talk. In that case it will take longer, but the added information might be very valuable.

Not every consumer, of course, will want to spend the time being interviewed. No problem. Plenty will. In most cases, people like to talk about what's important to them.

Arm your interviewers with clipboards. Following a brief introductory comment explaining the interview's purpose, ask icebreaker questions. Follow these with open-ended questions in which customers will tell the interviewer what supplier attributes are important to them and how they feel your organization is performing in each of those areas.

After asking the open-ended questions, interviewers can ask any specific product or service-related questions you want information on.

Interview Tips

Here are some tips on handling each of the customer satisfaction interview's four phases.

- **Introduction.** As a customer is preparing to leave your store, approach him or her and say, "We're trying to learn more about what our customers think of their experience shopping here. I wonder if you'd be willing to talk with me for a few minutes, just to answer a few questions about how well we're meeting your needs." (The interviewer might need to help the customer put her or his purchases in the car prior to conducting the interview.)

- **Icebreaker.** For a purchaser, a good icebreaker question might be, "I notice you bought some _____. How do you plan to use them?" (Following the respondent's answer, a tip on planting or fertilizing or some other aspect of caring for the product purchased is particularly helpful.)

  For the shopper who didn't make a purchase, the interviewer might say, "I notice you didn't buy anything today. Glad to have you here anyhow. Were you just browsing, or didn't we have what you were looking for?"

- **Open-ended questioning.** For both purchasers and non-purchasers, the following is a good way to approach open-ended questioning. "Did we have the products you needed? Were we able to answer your questions? Are there services we might have provided that we didn't make available? Please tell me about whatever's important to you in shopping here or at a similar place. Overall, how well would you say we met your needs today?"

Notice that even though some specific questions were asked here, they were example questions. The approach used here eases the customer into thinking in terms of supplier attributes he or she considers important.

Listen Carefully to Customer Comments

As you talk with the non-buyer, it's important to ask if she or he plans to go somewhere else to make a purchase. You can learn a lot about your competition that way, beginning with who your customers consider your competitors to be.

As the customer explains what supplier attributes are important to him or her, jot down the key words or phrases. You'll have to listen very carefully, writing as little as possible while making certain you've captured the key points. Once the respondent has told you which supplier attributes she or he considers most important, go back through the list, asking them to rank attributes in order of their importance.

Rank Attributes

A good way of doing this is to show the consumer the list, and ask him or her to place a "1" next to the most important item, a "2" beside the next most important item, and so forth. This is usually fairly easy for a respondent to do since there will typically be no more than five or six items on the list.

The next step is questioning the consumer about your company's performance in each attribute area. You can ask the person to rate performance in each attribute area using the familiar academic scale of "A" to "F." This is a scale that everyone understands. Shifting from numbers to letters emphasizes to the customer that this is a different process from ranking attributes.

Specific Questions to Ask Customers

It's likely that your organization will be seeking information from customers about products or services you are considering providing or changing and/or other specific aspects of your operation. Collect such information after the respondent has told you what supplier attributes she or he values and how your company is performing in each area.

Use a preprinted form to collect this information. A single sheet of paper, printed on both sides, works best.

On both sides of the paper, in the left column, list all the topics you want to ask about. Put them in short statements that are neither negative nor positive. For example, you might use "Employee product knowledge" or include "Employee courtesy."

Avoiding Pitfalls

You'll want to avoid the common pitfall of combining two separate attributes. It would be a mistake, for example, to say "Courteous and knowledgeable employees." Unless a customer happens to rate both attributes identically, you'll obtain unreliable responses with such combinations.

Other topics you might want to ask about include: quality of products offered, the range of product variety available, color choices in a particular product, your retail hours, the importance of having a giftware line, your store's layout, aisle width, lighting, adequacy of your parking area, checkout efficiency and others. You might include questions about a specific service you're considering adding or dropping.

The Core: a Customer Rating Scale

Ask the respondent to first rate the importance of each attribute on your list, using a scale of one to five with one being "extremely unimportant" and five being "extremely important."

After the customer has completed the importance rating of the attributes on the list, ask him or her to turn the sheet over and assess your company's performance in each area. Here you can use the same "A" through "F" rating scale used earlier in the open-ended questioning.

Use the Information You Collect

At the end of the interview, thank the respondent and be sure to ask, "Would you like to give me your name and address so we can put you on our mailing list?" You might add, "By the way, to show our appreciation for sharing your views with us, we'd like you to have _____." (This could be a 2-inch pot or some other item of limited value.) A week or so later, send the respondent a thank-you letter signed by both the interviewer and the president of the organization.

Using the information you collect is as important as the initial collecting. Circulate customer satisfaction information throughout your organization. Be sure to include bad news as well as good. In addition, make results of your ongoing customer satisfaction surveys integral to your company's strategic planning effort.

Customer satisfaction survey, Acme Garden Center

What's important to the customer?

Importance rating

Supplier attribute	Extremely important 5	4	Somewhat important 3	2	Extremely unimportant 1
Employee product knowledge	____	____	____	____	____
Employee courtesy	____	____	____	____	____
Product quality	____	____	____	____	____
Product variety	____	____	____	____	____
Range of color choices	____	____	____	____	____
Store hours	____	____	____	____	____
Giftware availability	____	____	____	____	____
Adequate parking	____	____	____	____	____
Aisle width	____	____	____	____	____
Adequate lighting	____	____	____	____	____
Checkout efficiency	____	____	____	____	____

Please rate our performance: A, B, C, D or F (A is most satisfying, F is least.)

Supplier attribute	Company performance
Employee product knowledge	_____
Employee courtesy	_____
Product quality	_____
Product variety	_____
Range of color choices	_____
Store hours	_____
Giftware availability	_____
Adequate parking	_____
Aisle width	_____
Adequate lighting	_____
Checkout efficiency	_____

155 Acres of Customer Service at Campbell's [3]

by Russell Miller

"I was coming from one of our growing greenhouses when I saw one of our sales people, a young girl, standing there looking out at the nursery," says Bob Campbell, owner of Campbell's Nurseries and Garden Centers in Lincoln, Nebraska. "There was a young woman looking at the nursery plants. So I asked the salesperson if she had waited on the young woman yet."

"She's just looking," she answered.

How to Make a Sale

"Let me show you how to make a sale," I said, and proceeded toward the customer. I passed the time of day for a few minutes and then asked her if I could answer any questions that she might have about our plants.

Her immediate reply was that they had a corner at home that they were trying to do something with and that she didn't know what kind of plant to put in this corner. "I asked her the size of plant she'd like, what kind of location was the corner, and I showed her a number of plants that would do well in that spot. All of a sudden she said, `You know, my husband likes spirea.'

"I told her that spirea would work perfectly, and for her to charge a potted spirea and take it home. If it didn't fit the bill, she could bring it back, and we would give her credit.

"I carried the potted shrub up to the counter, set it down, and told the salesperson to write up the sale on a charge ticket." Now the young lady comes back often—another permanent customer.

Service and Quality Equal Success

"Customer service makes this company successful," Bob says. And quality plants generate sale after sale, year after year. With this approach, the Campbell's staff has created an image of personal service that sticks in the customer's mind.

Bob says, "We never have the cheapest prices in town on plants and we don't strive to. People don't usually come to us for price, what they want is accurate advice to solve their problems.

"We probably have the most knowledgeable people in Nebraska working here. Many have been here for 10, 15 or 25 years, and 19 have degrees in horticulture." Of about 60 Nebraska Certified Nurserymen in the state, 14 are on Campbell's staff.

Bob's sons, Dick, Mike and Doug, are certified nurserymen, and along with his daughter, Sandy Priefert, direct specific operations at Campbell's. Dick is president of the company and heads the landscaping department. Mike and Doug, twin brothers, are company vice presidents. Mike is in charge of personnel and the garden centers, and Doug manages the work crews and nursery. Sandy, also a vice president, is office manager.

Select Employees Carefully

Mike says, "We try to take care of all our customers in the best way possible. We believe in one-to-one contact, and most of the time we want someone to be talking to a customer, even the old-time customers. It's this kind of service, our variety and quality of products, and our locations, that bring our customers back."

Mike is in charge of hiring new employees. Even though education and knowledge are important, he places a lot of emphasis on personality. "We want employees to do business the way we want to do business," he says, "especially if we want them to work with customers."

Knowledgeable Service: the Grower-Retailer's Advantage [4]

by Neal Catapano

You can beat Kmart in floral sales. How? Be different, define quality, share your knowledge. Look at plants from your customers' point of view. They want quality plants that will perform in their gardens with minimum care. The grower-retailer can drive a wedge at that one point that can loosen the mass merchandisers' hold on the market.

Don't Cut Corners

Start with varieties that are proven garden performers in your area. Go to field trials; conduct some of your own. There's a great deal of pressure on large wholesale growers to buy the cheapest seed or to grow cultivars that fill out quickly and bloom early regardless of whether the variety is really the best in the garden. Growers who never see the retail public are more likely to cut corners that may ultimately affect garden performance.

Make sure that every growing decision you make, from top to bottom, is with the ultimate goal of improving garden performance for your customers. Especially take care in using growth regulators. Excessive use can degrade garden performance.

Tie the whole thing together by promoting the idea at the retail level. Consumers will respond to the idea of buying the very best in garden performance from you, especially if you guarantee to replace any unsatisfactory plants.

Open to the Public

Don't underestimate the value of your growing facility as a selling point. People love going into greenhouses, seeing the plants, smelling the dirt and feeling the humidity. At Catapano Farms in Southold, New York, our entire growing facility is fully open to the retail public every day.

As people enter our range, their eyes widen in amazement as they see literally millions of bedding plants or thousands of poinsettias. We don't realize that the beauty we see every day is absolutely dumbfounding to the average person.

And don't underestimate *your* value to the retail public. Get out from behind the register on busy spring days, get into the selling area, and talk to customers. Who knows better about the plants you have and how customers can be successful with them than you?

Talking directly to people responsible for growing plants from start to finish and getting their expert advice is one service that will never be available at Wal-Mart. Your customers will also respond to dealing with the boss and enjoy interacting with a local family business. Involve yourself with your customers as much as possible; they are the lifeblood of your business.

Customer Service Is King in the '90s [5]

by Ann Turner Whitman

According to an executive with Bachman's chain of garden stores in Minneapolis, Minnesota, the customer is king in the 1990s. Their emphasis is on customer service and satisfaction. Bachman's trains their salespeople in product knowledge and sales approach and encourages them to do the little things, like listen, smile and say thank you.

Keeping staff motivated and interested in helping customers is crucial to good customer service. Dave Hamlen of Hamlen's Garden Center, Swanton, Vermont, and his staff regularly attend garden tours, trade shows and conferences during the slower months.

He also put six key staff people, including his landscape foreman and grower, through the Dale Carnegie course to help them communicate better with customers. It has paid off with increased staff confidence and customer satisfaction.

Customers Appreciate Smooth Checkout

Cash register procedures deserve special consideration because the experience that customers have here is the most lasting impression they will have of your business. Checkout should be smooth and efficient. The owner or manager should stay away from the cash register on busy days and spend his time helping customers nearby instead.

Chris Conant, co-owner and manager of Claussen's Florist and Greenhouse in Colchester, Vermont, says, "That was difficult to do at first, but I recognized that traffic flow was smoother when I stayed out of the cash drawer."

Chris also installed five telephone lines into his business and hired a knowledgeable staff person to handle calls nearly full-time during spring, answering customer questions. Chris claims that really makes a big difference to his operation's efficiency.

Service Is Where It's At [6]

by Julie A. Martens

At Terra Vista in Tulsa, Oklahoma, they went from lawn care to wholesale color production to retail sales. Their philosophy of customer service can spark some ideas for your own business.

Retail experts say customer service is king for turn-of-the-century shoppers. What's your angle on customer service? Kelly Keech, greenhouse manager, says, "Service is definitely where it's at. People want it, and I try to deliver.

"Every customer who enters the store is greeted. We ask, 'Is there anything I can help you find?' It's a much more positive question than 'Can I help you?' My current push is for the retail staff to get to know the customers personally and try to wait on them time after time.

"Parking is at a premium here, so the first thing we did was to pave the parking lot—that's especially important to women in heels and our older customers—and mark the parking spots. Because parking space is limited and we can't expand, the only way to fit as many cars as possible onto the lot is to make it clear where they go.

"We also check people out very quickly to free up those parking spots. We always have two or three people helping customers load their cars.

How do people carry their plants around the store? Do you have carts? "We use two things: boxes (like Coke boxes but with our name on them) and two-shelf carts. I learned that the average sale with a one-shelf cart is $30. With a double-decker cart, that average doesn't double; it goes up to $70 or $80!

"So, we bought a dozen two-shelf carts. Sales on those carts were so much higher we got another 12 the next year."

Do you offer any seminars or workshops for your customers? "What we're trying to do is make our customers knowledgeable and confident. Seminars and our bimonthly plant information newsletter help.

"Last fall we did a four-hour foliage plant seminar for two nights in a row. Seventy people attended.

"Our bonsai seminar had 80 people. Other successful topics have been a flea and tick day presented by Ortho, and a bulb fest featuring representatives from Abbot Ipco. I have also done presentations in office buildings over lunch hours."

Seminars Provide In-depth Customer Service [7]

by Peter Konjoian

There are two approaches to customer seminar series commonly used in our industry. The first and perhaps easier involves the seminar series that runs during the winter, usually on Saturday mornings. Attendance is usually free, and most sessions run for one hour.

These require less preparation than extended courses and are most often taught by the owner or an experienced employee. Sometimes local talents such as radio personalities or extension agents or newspaper columnists are invited to present seminars on topics with which they are familiar.

Tailor Topics to Clientele

Popular topics for this type of series include houseplants, African violets, roses, starting seeds indoors, bonsai and pest management. The list is endless and can be tailored specifically to your clientele. Ask your attendees what topics they are interested in learning more about—then offer them.

Here's a source of frustration that you need to avoid. If, during a seminar a specific product is recommended, make sure that you have an adequate supply on hand. Customers will be ready to buy after the presentation and will be quite exasperated if you run short. Worse yet, you may look foolish if you don't even carry the item.

It's important to communicate far enough in advance with seminar speakers, and ask them what products they will refer to and recommend during their seminar. Run specials on these items. The purpose of the seminar is to educate the customer and, at the same time, generate store traffic during an otherwise slow time of the year.

Include a Greenhouse Tour

A high point of our seminars and classes at Konjoian Greenhouses in Andover, Massachusetts, is to include a short, guided tour of our greenhouses. We have found that our customers love the "behind the scenes" look at commercial floriculture. Many of them will register for several topics and are amazed by the changes in the greenhouses from week to week. They also become a bit more aware of the work and effort involved in growing the plants they want to buy.

We provide coffee and doughnuts before the class starts. And plan on allowing extra time before and after the formal presentation for individual questions and conversation. Don't disappear right after the seminar to catch up on your watering.

We like to have people register in advance simply to help us plan for seating and refreshments. After a year or two you will learn what topics are popular and may not need to ask for registration. Ask your attendees how they heard about the seminar so that you learn what promotional efforts are most effective.

Advanced Seminars and Courses

The second type of seminar series is more of a course series than a seminar series and is the approach my family has chosen at Konjoian Greenhouses. We offer many multiple-week courses on topics that our customers have asked us to teach.

Individual courses last for one to five weeks, meeting on Saturdays at the greenhouses. Our Victory Gardens course, for example, met for five consecutive Saturday afternoons in March. Each class lasted two hours; the registration fee was $50.

Here is where the two approaches part company. The extended course must carry a fee to compensate the instructor and the business for time and materials. In the Victory Gardens course students receive seed, containers, bench space in the propagation house and space in a bedding plant house.

They return in late May to pick up their vegetable transplants. We think $50 is a bargain for all of the plants and information they receive.

Garden Preparation Course a Hit

The highlight of our series is the Garden Preparation Short Course, held on the first Saturday in May. This has become the talk of the town and runs for the whole day, including a barbecue lunch.

We draw from 40 to 50 people and offer split sessions throughout the day on topics such as soil preparation, perennial, container plantings, pest control, high tech gardening and a guided tour of our 20 greenhouses. The registration fee is $35, and people tell us it's a fabulous experience.

Don't Forget Tomorrow's Customer

Our seminar series doesn't stop with adult customers. We incorporate several activities for children in our yearly schedule. During the spring we encourage nursery and elementary schools to bring classes to the greenhouses for tours and planting sessions.

There are always extra plugs around, and the cost of the pots and soil are negligible compared to the community good will that is generated. Our local newspaper usually covers one or two of these sessions each year.

At a more advanced level we work with any junior high or high school student who comes to us with science project questions. If we get involved with the project in terms of materials and time, we will charge a small fee. Junior garden clubs have also scheduled tours and projects with us.

We have established a program in horticulture therapy recently with special needs classes in our area. Both elementary school as well as adolescent groups are involved and have enjoyed their experiences. We plan to have a few older students work part-time with us in the future.

Kill 'Em with Kindness

Massachusetts, as well as most of the Northeast, has been experiencing a sluggish economy. State budget deficits are climbing and are constantly in the news. I believe that if there ever was a time to concentrate on customer service, now is it. We have decided as a family to push our efforts to an even higher level. Turn it up a notch. Kill them with kindness.

Differentiating ourselves from our competition in this way is a decision that should help pave the way for continued success in the '90s and beyond. Being customer oriented instead of supply oriented is something we work hard at.

Pleasing Mrs. Persnickety [8]

by Dave Hamlen

Mrs. Persnickety is not your average customer. She's more critical than most. She is the kind of individual who makes most business owners cringe. Not that she won't part with her money, but she's hard to please. Despite her idiosyncrasies, she's valuable to your business. Let's look at how Mrs. Persnickety views where she shops and why she's valuable.

First, let's get to know Mrs. Persnickety. She takes great pride in her property, and gardening is her favorite hobby. She's active in the garden club and noted for her prize-winning plants. An orderly person, she expects orderliness in those with whom she does business. She wants quality.

Accidents Waiting to Happen

It's spring, and Mrs. P's gardening adrenalin is flowing. The weather's warm, the last frost date is past, and she's ready to plant. She heads to Pete's Petals to load up with plants to beautify her yard. But she arrives at Pete's to find the parking lot a zoo. Mrs. P. isn't the only one excited about the warm weather.

She'll be filling up the car, so she tries to park as close to the front door as possible. Mrs. P. notices there's no designated parking or anyone directing traffic, so she parks where she unintentionally creates a tight entrance/exit for Pete's. Now only one car can enter or exit at a time.

As Mrs. Persnickety heads toward the front entrance, she sees that Pete has a special on bagged bark mulch. It's piled high; some unsupervised children are sliding down the pile. One of then lands directly in front of Mrs. P., almost tripping her. Mrs. P.'s mother would never have allowed such a thing! But Mrs. P. is very determined and isn't going to allow some unruly children to spoil her day.

"Excuse Me, Do You Work Here?"

She breezes past the 35-foot-long waiting line at the cash register and enters the first greenhouse, where she spies some of Pete's famous begonias. The space between the benches is narrow, and Mrs. P. catches her coat on wire on the bench edge. It's an old coat, so she's not too concerned. The begonias aren't priced, and Mrs. P. has to track someone down.

She asks the first person who looks like an employee—it's another customer. She looks for five minutes and finds someone watering in one of the other greenhouses. He doesn't know the price but goes to find out. Five more minutes pass before Mrs. P. gets her answer.

It turns out the begonias are on special. Heading back to the begonias, she spots some double impatiens. She finds the price on a piece of cardboard, but has a hard time making it out—it's partially washed off. She wants to get at least a dozen impatiens and starts to look for a carrier. Pete is out of boxes, so Mrs. P. carries them six at a time to the register. There's no space for them, so she sets them in a corner and goes back for more.

No Space, No Prices, No Signs

Now that Mrs. P. has her impatiens, she heads back for her begonias. She has forgotten about the special price for 12 or more, so she gets only six. She tucks these also in the corner.

Back in the greenhouse things are busy. With the narrow aisles, she has a difficult time getting her other plants. She doesn't see any celosia, but rather than track someone down, decides to stop at Phil's Phlowers. Phil doesn't have Pete's selection, but his parking lot is bigger.

Mrs. P. wonders what new annuals Pete has this year. She'd like to try some of the All-America winners, if he has any. She asks to speak to Pete, but is told he has gone to get a new tire for the truck.

The person at the cash register sounds knowledgeable, but she's so busy Mrs. P. doesn't dare ask about All-America varieties. She makes one more pass through the greenhouse, picking up some white alyssum.

Heading back to her stash of plants in the corner, she finds someone has discovered them and taken three of her double impatiens. Mrs. Persnickety is finally infuriated. Gathering up her plants, she takes her place in the now 25-foot-long checkout line. While standing in line with nothing to do, she swears that this is the last time she ever shops at Pete's.

Improvised Discounts Cut Profits

As Mrs. P. approaches the cash register, she remembers something about the begonias on special. She dumps her plants on the counter and mentions this to the register person, who looks puzzled. She can see by the frown on Mrs. Persnickety's face she'd better make up a special.

Mrs. P. gets the begonias at 25 percent off—15 percent more than Pete intended. Mrs. P. doubts the register person's credibility, but is pleased to get 25 percent off.

At this point one of Pete's observant employees has noticed Mrs. P.'s car creating a traffic problem. He announces the car's make and license plate number over the intercom. Mrs. P. wants some potting soil, but after hearing that her car is in the way, decides to increase Phil's revenue instead.

It takes her three trips to the car to load her plants. She's sure everyone has singled her out as the parking violator. Mrs. P. starts backing out and almost collides with a car turning in. Mrs. P. figures this is the icing on the cake of her experience at Pete's.

On her way over to Phil's Phlowers, she thinks about what she just went through at Pete's and how it could have been more pleasant. Mrs. P. would like Pete to ask his customers what they think of his business. Perhaps a panel of customers could help Pete make their shopping experience more pleasant.

Where Can the Children Play?

Certainly, Pete's parking lot would be a good place to start. Designated parking or someone directing traffic on busy days could help with the congested parking. Mrs. P. can't understand why Pete devotes so much space to a pile of bagged bark mulch. She would rather see Pete's begonia special out front and labeled instead of a pile of bagged bark. She wonders if Pete is making the best use of his selling space.

Thinking about the children, she questions why Pete has never put in a children's sandbox or play area. Since present-day mothers lack the "responsibility" her mother had, Pete's play area could entertain the children while their mothers shop.

Mrs. P. hates waiting in line. She'd like to see Pete open up another cash register during busy times. Perhaps Pete could give people waiting in line something to do or read. Better yet, why not have people answer a gardening quiz? The person who answered everything correctly would get a prize when she got to the register. This would make the time go faster. Another thing Pete could do is provide information about his products and plants so people could be entertained and informed while waiting in line.

Make Shopping a Pleasant Experience

Mrs. P. glances down and notices the tear in her coat. Why are Pete's bench aisles so narrow? If he wants customers to buy, why doesn't he make it easy?

Mrs. P. would also like to see something exciting in the greenhouse. A display with a waterfall or fountain would be nice. Perhaps Pete could show customers how to combine various plants for a colorful display.

She then remembers the trouble she had finding out about the begonia special. A good, waterproof sign would have saved Mrs. P. time tracking someone down. Not only that, but the person watering could have stayed with the job. Mrs. P. and others would have bought more begonias had they known about the special. Why wasn't the cashier informed? This lack of communication costs Pete money.

Thinking of Pete's employees, she wonders why they don't wear some identification. It would make it easier to know who to ask for information and be less embarrassing for the customer.

Another thing Mrs. P. would like is boxes for her plants and carts to carry them in. She didn't like running back and forth between the greenhouse and the checkout and the car. She'd rather save her energy for planting.

Education Is Part of Your Price

One more idea for Pete would be a newsletter telling of new varieties and gardening tips. Mrs. P. would be glad to be on Pete's mailing list. She can't understand what was so important about getting a new tire for the truck. Did Pete have to do it himself? Why wasn't the person behind the register, who seemed knowledgeable, in the greenhouse where she could answer questions?

Mrs. P. would love to talk to Pete and tell him what his customers think about his business. It looks like she'll now vent her frustrations about Pete at Friday's garden club meeting.

The next time you see a Mrs. Persnickety at your business, walk up to her, shake her hand, and ask her what she thinks about your business. She may give you an earful. But this is the kind of information that will keep the Mrs. P.'s and other discerning customers coming back.

Customer Service Ideas for Super Sales [9]

by Steven and Suz Trusty

How many times have you walked through another greenhouse operation and seen a merchandising idea so simple and effective that you couldn't believe you weren't already using it in your business?

How many times have you visited with a long-time retailer/grower and picked up some hints and sales techniques for more efficient selling?

One of the most stimulating elements of business is observing other operations and sharing ideas. Both similarities and differences offer unlimited possibilities for growth and development of your business.

Adapting Ideas for Your Business

Every growing and retailing operation has its own unique atmosphere or personality. Each plant and product mix are chosen to appeal to a special customer base. One basic challenge of business operation is integrating new trends of an everchanging marketplace into viable merchandising tools to increase your own company's success.

You can dig up selling ideas wherever you are. Actively seek a sharing of information with other similar operations. As you do your own personal shopping, observe the merchandising techniques that affect your buying patterns. Determine how to adapt these ideas to your own business.

Color-Coded Tags

- At Suburban Lawn and Garden Inc., Overland Park, Kansas, plant material is identified and priced on plastic tags in colors that correspond to an informational sign. Although light requirement classifications may seem obvious, many customers previously had no idea how to determine this factor. This information can save many plants from a slow death in a poor location.

   Try to put yourself in the customer's position. Provide as much information as possible to guarantee his success with his plant purchases. This method is as helpful to the long-time customer hunting for an unusual plant as it is to the beginner choosing that first philodendron.

FIGURE 10. *Plant material is identified and priced on plastic tags in colors corresponding to those on this sign, which gives customers necessary light requirements for plants. Photo courtesy of Steven and Suz Trusty.*

Information Booth

- When the season is busy and knowledgeable employees are scarce, an easy-to-find information booth can greatly increase efficiency. Wall charts can list the most common plant material along with care instructions. Provide a wide selection of reference books and company-prepared planting and care guides.

  Rather than tie an employee to such an area on a full-time basis, you could put a phone in the booth. Customers can simply dial an indicated number, and an employee responds.

  Some questions can be answered on the spot. In other instances, an employee either comes to the booth or meets the customer at an agreed-upon location within the operation.

FIGURE 11. *During your busy season when knowledgeable employees are scarce, an easy-to-find information booth can increase efficiency. Photo courtesy of Steven and Suz Trusty.*

Planting Up Service

- Planting up containers is one customer service that every operation can provide. Allow adequate shelf or table surface, stock potting media in large bags or bulk, have a trash receptacle handy and keep the needed tools on hand.

  Customers may select the container and plant from available stock, bring in their own containers and select the plant, or select only the container and have an employee select the plant.

  If both the container and plants are purchased, the customer can be charged for the potting media used, but not the potting service. If the customer chooses to use his own container, a small fee may be charged for the potting service.

  Many customers may prefer to wait for their plants to be potted, so be sure to assign this task to an employee who won't feel pressured if someone wants to watch the work being done and ask questions about the plants and procedures. Some customers will choose instead to use this time to browse, frequently making additional purchases.

  If this service becomes so popular that you can't handle all requests at once, arrange a pick-up or delivery schedule to meet your customers' needs. Some kind of uniform identifying your employees will make it easier for your customers to get service when they wish it.

Put Customers First [10]

by Julie A. Martens

At McClish's Plants Plus Greenhouses in Washington Court House, Ohio, success comes in a six-month growing and selling period—from December to June. For Brent and Nancy McClish, a heavy retail emphasis makes the profit margin in their 14,000-square-foot production area.

Compete with Service, Quality

McClish's puts the customer first, offering an abundance of gravel for easy access, plant displays in the shade and plenty of parking. They also provide educational brochures about growing and take local school groups— typically 80 children at Mother's Day—on tour through the growing area.

"We can't compete with Kmart when it comes to hardgoods," Brent explains, "but we can compete on service and quality." Instead of carrying a large stock of hardgoods, for instance, Brent handles only materials they use themselves and provides explanations for use.

"Our goal is to sell everything we grow at our price," Brent says. "We're doing that by making our customers loyal friends. That's how we'll continue to be successful."

Moving Product In a Rural Setting

Retail sales account for 95 percent of McClish's business. The remaining 5 percent are wholesale transactions of hanging baskets with the local Kroger food store and several retail hardware businesses. "Many people push us to sell more wholesale," Brent says, "but we only do what we can produce ourselves, meeting our quality standards and within our time frame."

Two keys critical to their success are plant display and marketing. "We use displays that make the plants easy to see and easy to reach," Nancy explains. "All prices are clearly marked and everything is labeled."

Pricing Moves Product

Brent sees pricing as very important to moving product. "I offer volume discounts: individual bedding plant packs are priced a little higher than full flats," Brent says. Offering other products—cypress mulch, soil, seed or bulbs—in bulk also brings discounts to customers and sales for McClish's.

With the small growing area, customers can always count on working one-on-one with the owners and getting lots of personal attention. Mixed planters are popular with retail customers—especially on Mother's and Memorial Days—and Nancy's custom planting service makes planters-to-order convenient.

"If people can't find what they want in a preplanted planter, I'll put together a container mix to suit their taste," Nancy says. The most popular choices are a red geranium with white petunias, dracaena spike and sprengeri fern.

CHAPTER 6

Marketing

ADVERTISING

Wholesale-Gone-Retail Means Better Profits [1]

by Julie A. Martens

Tierra Vista Inc. started in 1984 from a well-known lawn maintenance company in Tulsa. They got into greenhouse growing in a big way right from the start with 55,000 square feet of production area, growing year-round color from plugs to finished product.

Today Tierra Vista is one of Oklahoma's premiere greenhouse operations that has a history as interesting as any *New York Times'* bestseller. The business grew out of an idea of a lawn care company executive, Ross Flood, who wanted to be able to supply all the various color needs of his lawn maintenance accounts.

Careful investigation of the greenhouse industry and guidance from DuPage Hort School graduate Kelly Keech supplied the momentum to start the business. Over time, sales direction took a 180-degree-turn from strictly wholesale to 100 percent retail. Company managers focused on creating a customer-driven business and an image that would be as well-known as the lawn care division of the business.

Success at Tierra Vista has grown out of some hard business decisions that considered profitability first. In a recent interview, Kelly Keech, now greenhouse manager, recounted how things got started and why the business has moved in the direction it has.

How did you generate interest in your product and find customers? "We put together a four-color flier to promote the business, got new trucks and hired a sales rep. That put us into the wholesale business. The problem with wholesale, though, was that growers outside the state could grow and ship product into our area cheaper than we could grow it in Tulsa. People would buy from us only as the out-of-state suppliers ran short of product.

"In the meantime, people kept stopping by, wanting to buy plants and look around the greenhouses. Our bottom line wasn't where we wanted it, and we decided we had to do something. So we went retail."

It sounds like you made the switch from wholesale to retail abruptly. Is that what happened? "No, not really. The first year we started retail we were doing about a 50-50 split, retail-wholesale."

Where did the final push to go 100 percent retail come from? "We saw how receptive the public was about coming into the greenhouse, and we looked at our bottom line figures. There's money in retail."

I've heard high praise for your retail operation. Who supplied the expertise? Is that one of your specialties? "We brought in a consultant from Colorado. The first thing he told us was to put in a wall of windows along 51st Street so people driving by could see the colors of the flowers.

"After that we added automatic doors with a canopy over them, so the entrance looked open and inviting. We invested in a four-color flier from the John Henry Company that we inserted into the newspaper and advertised on three key radio stations. The next thing we knew, we had to add more cash registers."

Some retailers swear by ads; others say they never advertise. Can you see sales benefits from your ads? "We do see people coming into the store with ads in hand, so we know they're working. When people think of flowers and plants, I want them to think of Tierra Vista. That's my goal. But no matter how much you advertise, in this business there are still sharp sales peaks throughout the year and equally sharp declines."

What's been your most successful promotion? "Garden trowels with a Tierra Vista sticker on them. We first offered them free with every $15 purchase; now they go with every $25 purchase. We gave away 8,000 this year. Our investment in them is only 50 cents."

What are your future promotion plans? Anything special? "I'm working to create an image of Tierra Vista in people's minds. I want people to think of us as their total retail source—for plants, for hardgoods, for information.

"I've contracted with a local radio personality to run broadcasts at the greenhouses, highlighting a crop and the things that happen in growing a crop to raise public awareness of growing and of the company.

"Image building doesn't happen overnight; it will be a long-term effect. The way I see it, though, we've already got advertising out there for us in the 52 lawn maintenance trucks. When people see those, I want them to think of the retail store on 51st Street."

It sounds like you have built a successful retail business that's on its way to becoming a local landmark. What's next, Kelly? "We're doing fewer of everything this year, concentrating on doing less better. Instead of 20,000 hanging baskets, for instance, we'll do 14,000. It's not that we've had poor quality in the past. I just think we can always improve the quality we're offering customers. That's a vital part of the Tierra Vista image."

Getting the Most from Radio [2]

by Russell Miller

During spring and holiday seasons, Steve Hall, The Wayne Greenhouse and Plant Market, Wayne, Nebraska, does daily, live talk shows over the telephone from his greenhouse. Sometimes he'll pose a question to listeners related to plants or gardening and rewards the winner with a free plant.

His live broadcasts, which began five years ago, often generate an enormous amount of customer traffic. He'll devote a half-hour to talking about the qualities of a certain plant—bougainvillea, for example. As a result, bougainvillea sales will likely increase within the hour and for six or more weeks afterward.

He also advertises in the "morning shopper" publication in Wayne with small ads, repeated often. "I think the same small ads running most of the time are better than large ads. It's the repetition that works. As long as we can keep up our quality, we don't have to compete for customers. I don't play the game of cheap prices for cheap plants; I deal in Cadillacs."

Direct Mail Keeps Customers Coming Back [3]

by Peter Konjoian

Five years ago, at Konjoian's Greenhouses, Andover, Massachusetts, we started a customer mailing list and began a direct mail campaign. We had 300 addresses in that first mailing. Today our list exceeds 5,000 addresses and has become the primary part of our advertising budget. The names on our list are of people who have been to our greenhouses in the past. We find it valuable to keep in touch with our regular customers at Easter, in the fall and at Christmas.

We have mailed one-page flyers, written newsletters, and sent colored postcards of our greenhouses in addition to plain postcards. The primary purpose of the mailings is to remind people of an upcoming season. We also announce scheduled courses and seminars.

We are now at the point where we want to expand our list to attract new customers to our business. Last spring we conducted a little market research with a survey that we designed and asked our customers to fill out. We gave them a bedding plant booklet for their efforts and hope to compile the data and define the demographic profile of our clientele. Then we will try to rent appropriate lists in our area and expand our customer base.

Trial Gardens, Open House Team Up for Sales

It takes little space to create trial gardens around your greenhouses. We started ours for the purpose of having living proof for our summer customers that flowers really do last all season long with proper care. We also use the gardens to trial new offerings and help make production decisions. With all the cultivars available, outdoor trials provide valuable information.

A word of caution is necessary, however, because the gardens take quite a bit of effort and care. If you don't have the time to tend to them, the idea could backfire, resulting in poorly kept beds that fail to impress anyone. Spend some money on drip irrigation and tap into your constant feed lines in the greenhouse to help out.

Take advantage of your effort by holding an open house during mid to late summer. Publicize it and have refreshments and maybe even a door prize or raffle to make it exciting. Use it to show some new design ideas or color schemes. Encourage people to make notes for next year and have cultivars labeled clearly. Lastly, keep your fingers crossed for nice weather.

Elective Advertising: Key to Reaching a New Market [4]

by Russell Miller

"At Campbell's Nurseries and Garden Centers in Lincoln, Nebraska, our business is built on the fact that we have many knowledgeable people. I stress to customers that we are a family business—all of us have one or two degrees from the University of Nebraska—because people like that," says Bob Campbell. Pictures of the employees are in the Campbell's catalog and in ads to stress this point.

Bob designs his own newspaper ads that run in one daily Lincoln newspaper and a country-farm trade newspaper south of Lincoln. "We're trying to reach a larger market, especially the rural areas," Bob says.

Adding Ads

"I'm starting to run more ads, but on a smaller basis; 10-inch and 25-inch ads three times a week instead of larger ads less often during the week. The cost is the same, but we get more exposure. During the Christmas season and spring, I'll run ads on Tuesday, Thursday, Friday and Saturday, avoiding the days when a lot of food ads from shopping centers appear. I always keep the ads in the same format so that they are easily recognized."

For the past 35 years during the spring, Bob presents three- or four-minute daily, non-paid, gardening advice spots on one radio station. He calls it a public service because it's free, and he's not allowed to mention the Campbell's name on the air. During the Christmas season, Bob's paid radio commercials are heard eight times a day on three radio stations. He targets each one for a different audience: the early morning, midmorning, late morning drivers, for example. He also advertises on television but only during the Christmas season.

Bob says he spends between 3 and 5 percent of his gross sales volume on advertising throughout the year, but during "anything special, like Christmas, I'll spend at least 5 percent."

Making "News" Happen [5]

by Kathleen Pyle

If you're starting up a greenhouse operation with shoestring finances and more ingenuity than capital, then look to Joel Olson, owner of Hillview Greenhouses, LaCrosse, Wisconsin, for inspiration. Joel and his wife Jean bought their 15,000-square-foot greenhouse four years ago for a fire sale price.

Maximizing Production Space

At Hillview Greenhouses, a 75 percent retail operation, variety is the theme. According to Joel, who propagates almost everything himself, "We offer too much variety, more than we should." He grows bedding plants for spring sales but has also expanded his product line to make limited production space pay off year-round.

Every Customer Counts

Although he's trying to build up business with mass merchandisers, Joel would like to see Hillview go 100 percent retail. "I enjoy spending some time talking with every customer," Joel says, emphasizing they can count on the store's caliber of personal service. Not surprisingly, his monthly radio broadcast is called *Friend to Friend*. Listeners call in with their gardening questions, and Joel shares his expertise. He also does television advertising, finding it to be the most effective promotion for this business.

Joel relies on seasonal promotions to draw more customers into the store. At Christmas, the local girls' choir sells poinsettias for him. Hillview kicks off the spring season with an open house on May 1. In summer, Joel offers one item every day for half price.

Natural Predator Press Release

Joel isn't shy about exploiting media opportunities. A few years ago he decided to try natural predators in the Hillview greenhouse and alerted the media with a press release. The local TV station showed up to witness him releasing ladybugs—the unobliging insects flew straight at the television cameras! Pests ended up out-reproducing the predators, Joel laughs, and he now uses a pulse fogger.

Signs Are Advertising, Too [6]

by Russell Miller

Educating the consumer about how to care for the quality plants they purchase has become a top priority at Caan's Flowers at Waldheim, a family business in Sheboygan, Wisconsin.

A few years ago, Greg Parmley (former co-owner) created a perennial display garden on one side of the business. When the perennials went in, so did **informative signs** describing the plants and how to care for them.

"Sales began to increase dramatically," Greg says. "Signage is a very important part of our business." Now there's an emphasis in creating signs that direct the flow of customer traffic both inside the greenhouses and around the outdoor plantings.

Next spring, customers will also get a **descriptive map** of the greenhouses and the surrounding display areas. They show where to locate the plants and give tips on how to select the right plant for home. Owner Tom Caan also plans to have "street signs" posted to assist customers.

Changes Create Interest

Also next spring, a **30-foot totem pole** will be placed near the entrance to Caan's. It features a thunderbird with a 10-foot wingspan and, like all true totem poles, describes an Indian legend. "It will be a Sheboygan landmark," Greg says. "We change something at the business every year to create customer interest."

FIGURE 12.
Informative signs describing the plants and their care combine advertising with customer service.

From April through June they **advertised on a billboard** on a main thoroughfare between their north and south stores. They also advertise on an easy-listening radio station on weekends and in the local newspaper, and they are considering developing a four-color brochure as an insert for the paper.

"We want to inspire our customers every day with some sort of advertising. We want them to visit us regularly," Greg says. "We have an extensive **advertising campaign** with something in the newspaper every week. It has a big impact on our customers."

Christmas Headquarters

In the fall most of the retail area is decorated for Christmas. "We go the whole 9 yards," Greg says. "Everyone here really kicks in for Christmas!" The flower shop, with a new 12-foot by 24-foot walk-in display cooler, becomes Christmas headquarters, where virtually the widest and most **unique selection of holiday items** in the area can be found.

"Everything is done with personalized attention," Greg says, "from an elegant center piece to a huge specimen poinsettia." Santa Claus visits with children, and Mrs. Claus serves hot apple cider and cookies.

Retail Requires Imagination [7]

by Julie A. Martens

Claussen's Florist & Greenhouse, Colchester, Vermont, operates on a 50-50 split between retail and wholesale on a year-round basis, but retail takes the lead in spring sales, with sales continuing into August. A vigorous advertising effort keeps Claussen's in the public eye, with weekly, **two-color newspaper ads** and weekly, 30-second **radio spots.**

Weekends at the Colchester site create tricky traffic patterns. The garden center sits on a two-lane city street one block past a busy intersection; traffic jams are an hourly event. Chris Conant, owner-manager, tackled this problem by using maintenance personnel to direct cars, extending business hours and offering special senior citizen discounts on Mondays.

"Extending our hours (open daily until 8 p.m. from April 15 to July 1) increased sales dramatically for existing and new clientele. The evening hours also help spread the weekend crowd across the week," Chris explains. "Mondays are phenomenal—they're as busy as weekend days with the senior specials."

Getting customers into the retail store is just one part of the sales equation. The second part involves a **detailed map** of the retail area, indicating bench numbers, product and prices. "The map also serves as a promotional piece for in-house specials," Chris says.

It Pays to Advertise [8]

by Roy A. Larson

My wife and I were returning to Raleigh after attending the Seeley Conference in Ithaca, New York, and I treated her to lunch at a fast food restaurant near Richmond, Virginia. When we walked into the restaurant, we saw a couple wearing t-shirts with the word "Yoder" printed on them, and the fellow also had a Yoder cap.

I strolled over to their table and asked them if they were affiliated with Yoder Brothers. They proudly said they were and asked if we'd seen their 18-wheeler truck when we drove into the parking lot. They were excited about the truck, not only because it was new, well-equipped and comfortable, but also because it was very attractive. After we finished eating, we went out to the parking lot where I saw a shiny trailer with paintings of flowers conspicuously displayed, as well as the company logo and purpose.

That luncheon stop affected me three ways: My attitude about the value of company t-shirts, caps and other articles of clothing was affirmed, my thoughts about the value of promoting floral products was reinforced, and my hunger was overcome.

Clothing Advertises, Too

There are several positive things to write about wearing clothes that identify the firm for which you work. When I put on a cap, shirt or jacket with the North Carolina State University logo, it shows that I'm pleased to be affiliated with the institution.

Clothing with a company logo is good advertising, as long as the clothing is clean and whole, not faded, torn or dirty. One interiorscaping firm in Charlotte, North Carolina, attracted new clients because its employees wore clothing identifying them with the company. Clients appreciated the cleanliness and company identification.

Many times **clothes become conversation pieces**—someone recognizes the name because a relative or friend works there, or maybe they've even bought some of the floral products. My Yoder example is typical. I saw the name on the t-shirts and cap and struck up a conversation with the couple—Tom and Nancy Martin from Pendleton, South Carolina. They've been working for Yoder Brothers for five years, and they praised the company.

I mentioned the episode to Ramsey Yoder when I saw him at the Ohio Short Course, and he was equally complimentary about the Martins' dedication and competence. None of that discussion would have taken place if Darlyne and I hadn't seen the Yoder t-shirts and cap.

Your Truck Is Your Ad

The other effect I mentioned at the beginning of this article pertains to **decorating vehicles** in a way that promotes floriculture. The Yoder 18-wheeler not only advertises the company, it also calls attention to flowers. The truck begins its weekly journey in South Carolina, goes to North Carolina, then over to Virginia, and finally completes its trip in Maine.

It's hard to guess the number of travelers and residents who are reminded about flowers when that attractive semi travels along some of the most densely populated areas in the eastern United States. That mobile billboard may prompt many people to buy plants or floral arrangements as gifts or for themselves.

Coming down on the same highway a month later, we were passed by an 18-wheeler owned by one of the largest flower shippers in the East. The name of the company was inconspicuous on both the door of the cab and on the trailer. I'm aware of the vital service that that the company provides the floral industry, but its significance was probably lost on most of the people who saw it.

The Professional Plant Growers Association began giving landscaping awards years ago. Perhaps some floral organization could recognize companies for having the most effective designs on their vehicles, ranging from florists' mini-vans to large 18-wheelers. Advertisements are no longer allowed along some highways, but I don't know of any regulations that forbid a "moving" highway advertisement.

Television Wins Every Time [9]

by Russell Miller

"Anyone can carry or grow a petunia, but selling it is a whole different thing," says Tom Pasco, owner of the Flower Farm in Pasco, Washington. "We adapt what other people are doing regarding advertising. In all areas of our business, we like to do what successful people do. We approach marketing in the same way. Advertising and promotion are important to the success of many businesses."

It's ironic, he adds, that so many people in the industry limit their advertising budget to 3 percent of their sales. "Individual companies in other industries utilize 30 to 40 percent of their budget in advertising. Why can't we at least spend 10 percent? Advertising is an investment in our future. Our advertising budget represents 7.5 percent of our sales, and we are moving closer to 10 percent this year."

Immediate, Long-term Results Important

He says you have to **look at advertising in two ways.** Both the immediate return on advertising and the long-term results are important. "The question you have to ask yourself is, 'How much am I willing to invest in future sales? Not just tomorrow's sales, but for sales next year, five years from now and sales for every year you plan to remain in business?'"

Tom and Gayle have tried coupons and advertising on radio but were not pleased with the results. Now they are advertising heavily with weekly full-column ads in the daily newspaper—but **television commercials impress them the most.**

"We advertise with 30-second commercials on all three of our local network TV stations. In the spring and summer we come on every weekday right after the local news and before the network news. This provides us with tremendous coverage."

TV Advertising Is Cost Effective

Television advertising is relatively inexpensive for their area, Tom says. It's even cheaper in the long run than newspaper advertising. "Five TV commercials weekly actually cost less than one weekly newspaper ad." He says growers in larger communities, however, may not find TV advertising as inexpensive as they do because the prices for buying air time may be a lot higher.

"I put together our ads in the newspaper and on TV. You can't have advertising people putting together your ads, otherwise your ads end up looking like everyone else's ads. This way, our ads are distinctive. I appear in the TV commercials, talking with the viewers, face-to-face, from the Flower Farm."

People Know Where to Find Me

"People see my face on TV day after day, and after awhile they begin to feel as if they know me like their next-door neighbor—and they always know where they can find me. When they come to the Flower Farm, they feel very comfortable talking with me and asking questions.

"We continue **advertising through the fall and winter** to reinforce interest. It's repetitive advertising in effect and very much like subliminal advertising—no one forgets our name."

Coupons and Community Involvement [10]

by Julie A. Martens

If you move into a home in St. Charles, Illinois, you'll probably be greeted by the Welcome Wagon, a collection of samples and discounts from local merchants. Among the collection are coupons from L & M Greenhouses for discounts off spring bedding plants, fall garden mums, Halloween pumpkins or Christmas trees.

"Over 10 percent of our Welcome Wagon coupons are redeemed," says Mike Clesen, co-owner of L & M, "and most of those people come back again as regular customers." Lynn Clesen, the "L" of L & M, agrees that the Welcome Wagon advertising is very effective. "Coupons in the newspaper with our regular ads just don't work," she says. "The best advertisement is stopping by and looking around or by word of mouth."

Making a Mark in the Community

Mike and Lynn are popular with 4-H Club members, who ran a haunted house in an 80-foot hoop house at the greenhouses last year and who often present seminars at L & M during special Mother's Day anniversary celebrations.

Targeting Your Customers With Direct Mail [11]

by Mary Lu Parks

For direct mail to be successful, the three most important elements are the mailing list, the mailing list and the mailing list.

Even if your advertising message is compelling, timely and creatively crafted, the package cannot overcome a bad mailing list. All your efforts and money may be wasted if your list is old, out of date, or inadequately targeted to reach your market.

The proper selection of a mailing list depends on knowing the demographics of your customers—interests, age, sex, income, lifestyle, etc. Simply put:

- Who do you want to reach?

- What do you want to say?

- What do you want them to do?

With this information in mind, look for a list that will reach your market at the right time.

Consider these options: You can **create your own mailing list,** you can **rent a list,** or you can **include your message with others in co-op mail.** Read how three growers selected and successfully implemented their mailing lists.

Lone Star Growers Uses Team Effort

"We went to direct mail because it gave us better results," says Susie Smith, former marketing coordinator for Lone Star Growers, San Antonio, Texas. As wholesalers, Lone Star sells annuals, native plants and nursery stock to garden centers, mass markets, landscape contractors, municipalities and highway departments. Lone Star mails a monthly plant availability list to customers and prospective customers.

A quarterly newsletter is also mailed to a bigger list that includes schools and extension agents. It describes new plants, plant uses, tips for planting and maintaining plants, plus a calendar of native plant events. Because of the newsletter, Susie says customers are "more responsive and better informed."

"It's a challenge for any business to keep its list updated," says Lynn Turner, former administrative assistant. At Lone Star, it's a team effort with several departments cooperating. The computer department maintains the list while customer service, sales representatives and the credit department monitor the list to add prospects and eliminate those who are not potential buyers. Address corrections are requested for each mailing. Their established policies and procedures ensure regular corrections and a quality list.

Outside Computer Service for Mailings

Charlie Fischer is an African violet enthusiast whose company has marketed violets by mail order for 40 years. His four-color catalog lists 175 cultivars of Saintpaulia and Gesneria, along with all the supplies a violet hobbyist could want. A mailing list of 15,000 is maintained by an outside computer service. "It pays to have your labels generated on a timely basis," Charlie says.

Fischer Flowers, Linwood, New Jersey, used to keep the mailing lists in-house using an old Addressograph system, but according to Charlie, "it got away from us," and they decided an outside service would work better.

Fischer's list is compiled from the membership of Gesneriad and Saintpaulia Associations plus names of their mail order purchasers. Additional names are obtained from the Philadelphia Flower Show where Fischer has exhibited violets for 40 years. More names result from a brisk walk-in business at their Linwood greenhouses. Updates, corrections and deletions are done on a regular basis.

Mail order is 10 percent of Fischer's gross sales, but it continues to increase. "We see mail order as an area for growth," Charlie says.

Mailing Lists Rented, Not Sold

If you are interested in renting a mailing list, look in the Yellow Pages under Mailing Lists or Mailing Services. For additional help in selecting a list to meet your objectives, look under Mailing Services, Letter Shops or Advertising—Direct Mail. Many of these companies will broker lists, and they can also be quite helpful in finding the best list for you.

List rental is usually for one-time use. The list owner will request a sample of what you plan to mail and when you want to mail it. Most lists are salted with decoys to detect misuse, and you are restricted from adding names to your own mailing list file.

Lists are rented, not sold, because the owner has a great deal of resources invested in the list. Lists are proprietary products and misuse constitutes a criminal or civil offense in most states. Those who abuse list rental can be sued for misappropriation of confidential information, theft of trade secrets, compensatory damages, unjust enrichment, or criminal liability.

Kaisers Retail Goes Co-op

Co-op mail offers the greatest economy for direct mailers. Your advertising message is mailed along with others who share the cost of printing, postage and handling. There are many local options available.

Jackie Schach, owner of Kaisers Greenhouse and Flower Shop, has used Val-Pak co-op mailing for 10 years in the Cleveland, Ohio, area. She finds co-op mail to be "very effective . . . it pulls people in." She schedules Val-Pak three to four times a year on a seasonal basis with special offers on the coupons. Her service rep has been helpful in selecting trade areas to target, and she likes the fact that her retail shop will be the exclusive flower shop represented in her selected mailing areas.

Val-Pak does co-op mailing in more than 300 metro areas in the United States and Canada. You can find Val-Pak in the Yellow Pages under Advertising—Direct Mail, or call (800) 237-6266 to locate this service near you.

In 14 western states, the U.S. West Bell companies will put your insert in their phone bills. The bill insert program is called Teleride. Call your local telephone company business office to see if this is available in your area.

The simplest, closest-to-home co-op program is mailing stuffers or inserts with your own invoices. Don't overlook this economical direct mail solution.

The goal of all direct mail is to evoke response—you want calls, visits, inquiries and sales. Your message should be interesting and must go to the right person to be effective.

So, whatever the source of your mailing list, remember to choose carefully or meticulously build and maintain your own. A clean, up-to-date, accurate, targeted mailing list is the key to results. Here's wishing you many happy returns!

How to Get Them in the Door and Keep Them There [12]

by C. Anne Whealy

Humber Nurseries, Brampton, Ontario, prints a four-color catalog annually. They distribute their 50,000 catalogs through the mail and newspapers. Ads in the Saturday papers also have proved to be successful. Flyers are sent out to various areas with color-coded coupons to determine the areas of greatest response. Humber also sponsors a Saturday morning radio gardening program and supports local horticultural groups and service clubs as a public relations gesture.

Cullen Country Barns, Markham, Ontario, also prints a four-color catalog. The 750,000 catalogs are distributed through the newspaper. Barry Benjamin, manager of Cullen, uses the catalog to create bedding plant excitement. "We always wonder what we are going to do next year to create interest."

New Varieties Are the Industry's Salvation

"You have to have new varieties, you just can't sell the same thing over and over. The retail grower has the greatest potential because he can try anything new he wants. He can create his own new products," Barry says.

Humber's main attraction is the greenhouses. Their logo is "Buy from a Grower . . . Buy the Best." "From a retail merchandising aspect, people like to wander through greenhouses and buy from a grower," says Humber's Frans Peters. "People will come here in January, February and March just to watch everything grow. Growing really appeals to people, and it makes them want to come back. Seventy percent of our customers are repeat, 20 percent are word of mouth and the other 10 percent come from advertising."

For promotions, Humber offers a "pak" of the week, Ladies' Day on Wednesdays and Senior Citizens' Day on Thursdays. Wednesdays at Cullen Country Barns is 10 percent off on bedding plants for everybody.

Product Display Is Critical

The details of effective display are important to both retailers. Time is spent replacing plants to make full packs, arranging colors attractively, keeping varieties straight and maintaining an orderly display. Raised benches are used so that nothing is displayed on the ground.

At Cullen, the benches are stacked toward the back to give a vista of color, with baskets tiered so that their tops can be seen. The annuals are delivered to a back door and brought in on racks. Cullen owns some racks, while other growers lend their racks, which they drop off full and pick up later when empty.

Merchandising, through retail area appearance and proper presention of product, has paid off for Humber and Cullen. And both Frans and Barry agree, if the front bed looks good then the customer's first impression will be favorable.

At Humber, the production greenhouses are also the display greenhouses, and feature several outdoor display areas. "We have a perennial trial area for new products. If they perform well and we like them, then we sell them. People like to see what these plants will do in the landscape,"

FIGURE 13. *An attractive retail area appearance and proper product presentation does pay off. Photo taken at Fisher's East, Reynoldsburg, Ohio.*

says Frans. "When we display baskets, we have a lot of 5-inch baskets nearby so they can make their own. We make displays in the building too, because not everyone wants to walk through the greenhouses."

Educate Your Customer

"If you can make the product attractive and appealing to the consumer, help them and give them information, you will be successful. Try to steer them in the right direction. It's the retailer's obligation to educate his customer," Barry says.

"We use informational signs and offer *Green Thumb Guides* (information sheets) because people want to know, and it's important to give your customers the right information," says Frans. "We have to hire part-time salesmen who don't know everything, so they give customers the guides. People are interested in learning, and we have a library here—actually a bookstore. People come to study and to buy books."

COMPANY IMAGE

Gardening Solutions Mean Repeat Customers [13]

by Douglas Green

After redefining the business in the late 1980s, Simple Gifts Farm Greenhouses, Athens, Ontario, Canada, saw annual sales increase over 60 percent in both 1988 and 1989. This redefinition was the result of my wife, Andrea, and I attending a business marketing course.

It involved changing the nature of our business from that of a "seller of plants" to "a business dedicated to helping other gardeners solve gardening problems." This emphasis on problem solving allowed our marketing plans to be much broader based and to focus on retailing aspects that may not be considered in the average greenhouse business.

Surveys indicated the most important thing customers want is information. Creating a marketing policy based on providing that information spawned a total signage program in the nursery, a newspaper gardening column, a newsletter, a spring gardening seminar and a speakers' service to non-profit community groups.

Provide Information

The first, and constant, priority is information for customers in the greenhouse sales area. All plants—annuals, perennials and woody ornamentals—have signs describing cultural habits, height, light requirements, bloom color and bloom time, as well as several suggested uses.

While some signs are available commercially, signs for unusual plants—we grow over 900 varieties of perennials—have to be done every year by hand. Producing the signs is time consuming (about 36 hours of labor each spring), but the minimal cost of each 7- by 11-inch plastic sheet (46 cents per sheet) has wonderful customer service benefits. The signs increased sales and jogged the memory of tired staff when confronted with questions about the plant. Plant data is stored on computer, and from this we get our catalogs, staff reminders and work sheets for sign making.

Newspaper Column Is an Investment

A second customer information source is our newspaper gardening column that reaches approximately 60 percent of our customer base on a monthly

FIGURE 14. *Customers want information—signage in your greenhouse sales area should be a priority. Photo taken at Fisher's Greenhouse, Columbus, Ohio.*

or weekly basis. The hour or two a month we spend writing is well invested in our customers' satisfaction and awareness of our business.

Joining the Garden Writers Association of America (10210 Leatherleaf Court, Manassas, Virginia 22111) will bring media news releases from different horticultural companies, giving any writer enough ideas to keep a 300-word monthly column well filled. Otherwise, simply writing about the questions you receive during a business day is a good starting point.

Beginning with a single monthly paper, our articles now also appear in two locai weekly papers, and we've received a request from an editor in a nearby city for a third weekly. Newspaper editors assure us that the gardening column is one of their most popular features.

Newsletter Educates Customers

Each spring, customers are invited to fill out a name and address form that is their subscription to a gardening newsletter. The quarterly newsletter is not used as a blatant sales tool featuring ads and products, but rather aims to educate about plants, products and techniques that help gardeners solve problems. While we do stock every product we write about, the emphasis is on problem solving, not selling a product.

The four-page newsletter costs approximately 6 cents each for all the writing, commercial layout, printing and folding. Stuffing and stamping envelopes costs another 6 cents per piece. Canadian postal rates are 39 cents per envelope, so each newsletter costs us 51 cents.

At this rate, we spend $1.53 (Canadian) per customer per year on customer maintenance via the newsletter. On the assumption that it's cheaper to hold a customer than get a new one, we think the newsletter is a good idea as it reminds our customers of our plants and services during the off seasons.

Computerized Mailing List Is Important

The computerized mailing list generated by the newsletter provides a clear picture of where our customers live. By mapping each household, we can identify neighborhoods in which our advertising is working. Custom-designed mailing flyers are sent directly into those neighborhoods.

Upper income neighborhoods are also being targeted with this direct mailing approach. Market penetration becomes crystal clear when comparing a customer list to a postal census. The return rate of customers from year to year (a measure of customer loyalty) shows up dramatically when we update the mailing list. While our data is only three years old, we have documented the increasing rate of customer loyalty in our customer base. Decreasing rates of customer loyalty would be a fast indicator of problems in the business, regardless of cash intake.

Seminars Pull in Customers

We started a spring seminar in 1989 and repeated it the following year, because over 97 percent of the people attending the first seminar returned in the spring to purchase plants and garden supplies.

We start planning for the seminar six months before the date by booking the hall and speakers. We choose speakers based on current gardening trends and community interests. For example, this year is the local town's centennial, and there are gardening contests based on 19th century plants. We arranged for the horticultural curator of Upper Canada Village, an historical research and demonstration village of early Canadian living, to speak.

Selecting Topics

The last two winters have been very hard on rose survival here in eastern Ontario, so the horticulturist responsible for the Royal Botanical Gardens' rose collection shared his expertise on winter survival. Other speakers included a commercial lawn care operator who uses organic techniques, and Andrea—a trained artist—discussed gardens as art. I talked about easily grown perennial flowers. Once you start thinking about the events going on around your business, the problem is not having enough to talk about, but restricting the number of talks to give.

Each speaker costs us approximately $75 to $100 for the day. We use institution-sponsored outreach programs or take advantage of business friendships. We also provide lunch and first class treatment for our speakers (for example, a gift of a $25 cheese basket). Spoil your speakers: There's a network among speakers that will work to your future advantage.

Advertising is done through newsletter and newspaper articles, so there are no direct advertising costs. Hall costs, slide projector rentals and a full coffee pot are other costs. We find that asking participants to bring a brown bag lunch works well, and the gardening conversations around the long lunch tables add to the friendly atmosphere we are trying to create.

A Fee Equals Commitment

Total costs for this year's seminar will be $350. Customers are asked to pay $5 each, which more than covers costs incurred. Our experience is that having to pay a minimal charge increases customer attendance and commitment. While the Christmas newsletter indicates the seminar date, final details are sent out one month before in the spring newsletter.

On the day of the seminar we have several people there to greet newcomers, take registrations, print name tags, serve coffee, set up projectors and see that speakers are comfortable and have no last minute requirements. We do our best to run on time and find that most people appreciate this.

Become a Speaker's Bureau

Wouldn't you be more inclined to shop at a store where you personally knew the owner? One way we try to meet new customers individually is by acting as a gardening speaker's bureau. Both Andrea and I talk to community groups, presenting slide shows, discussing gardening problems and providing solutions.

All newsletters mention our speaker's bureau. We give approximately 25 different talks each year to a variety of community and church groups. This is largely a donation of time, but most groups will thank the speaker with a small gift or a check to cover gas expenses.

Allowing enough time after a speech to answer questions lets you become the "expert" and make new customers. Community groups are hungry for speakers, and polished speeches aren't necessary. If a retail greenhouse owner can survive the questions during May, he or she can easily survive a short speech and question period during February.

Slide Sources

The basis for our speeches is an extensive slide collection of flowers and gardens that is constantly being updated. Those who don't use cameras can obtain good slide shows from the Professional Plant Growers Association or Ohio State University. These are reasonably priced and can be used for several different talks.

If you are taking your own photos, we suggest shooting gardens early in the morning or late in the evening, with the slowest speed film available. The use of filters is necessary when shooting outdoors, and a polarizing filter should always be used to intensify colors.

Blue graduated filters eliminate the tendency towards washed-out skies in slides, and other graduated filters such as orange or tobacco, warm up autumn scenes in a spectacular manner. Blue and purple flowers don't appear truly blue on normal slide film, but this problem can be solved by using an 82A filter. Inexpensive close-up lens attachments will allow you to shoot some truly impressive pictures.

Slide Shows Help Structure Talks

A slide show can help you structure your talk. You don't need to memorize or write a long speech. Arranging a few slides in logical order (I prefer alphabetically), and talking about them as the slides come up on the screen is a fast way to create a presentation.

I plan about one slide per minute of talk, so a 15-minute presentation will have between 15 and 20 slides. For the truly tongue-tied among us, try a slide show with a taped commentary, video tape or computer animation. Then you can simply answer questions to complete the presentation. We find that a speaker's bureau definitely generates retail business, and having met us, many people become loyal customers.

Our marketing program development is never really finished. We do customer surveys every year. For the future we plan a cable television gardening show and increased use of computer generated graphics. Providing gardening solutions is our business purpose, so you can bet we'll do our best to keep up with our customers.

An Image of Quality and Fairness [14]

by Russell Miller

Steve Hall of Wayne, Nebraska, believes quality, not price, is the best reason customers should come to your retail greenhouse. At The Wayne Greenhouse and Plant Market, quality sells the product. "You never have to worry about the competition if you can beat them on quality," he says. "With quality plants you can pick your price."

The population of Wayne is about 5,200, yet it's one of the largest communities in northeastern Nebraska. "The population of Nebraska is about 1 ½ million, so there's not a lot of customers to attract," Steve says.

"We do everything we can to get customers and then get them back again and again."

The business has two locations: a flower shop and glass-covered greenhouse in Wayne and The Wayne Greenhouse Plant Market, an 11,000-square-foot Stuppy greenhouse built in 1983, 1 mile east on the outskirts of Wayne. The original Wayne Greenhouse is used for both retailing and growing cut flowers. The greenhouse also supplements the crops grown for retail at The Plant Market, where several double inflated poly hoop houses are used to grow bedding plants and pot crops for retail and wholesale.

Quality Deserves Top Dollar

Nearly all bedding plants are sold at retail. "There're no mixes. We keep all varieties separate. No one else I know does it this way, but it's one of the reasons customers come here."

At The Wayne Greenhouse Plant Market, Steve decided to eliminate end-of-season sales, an idea he wishes would sweep the industry. "About three years ago we decided never to lower our prices on anything again. It's one of the smartest things we ever did. Customers used to wait until Memorial Day for a sale to come in and buy, and then one year it didn't happen.

"Everybody learned pretty fast," he adds. "I heard a lot of comments, but surprisingly some ladies liked it. They felt it was fair. So we put up a sign behind the sales counter at the beginning of each spring season that reads: 'In fairness to our early customers, there will be no end-of-season price reductions.' We have to watch and plan our crop numbers more, but it's still worth it. I'd rather throw away seedlings than throw away finished plants because they didn't sell."

A Strong Community Image [15]

by Julie A. Martens

Elliott's Greenhouses & Garden Centers combines wholesale and retail sales at a growing/retail location in Lyndon Center, Vermont, and a second retail site in Stowe. Customers and commercial accounts come from a 75-mile radius. Business has been strong over the years, and manager Steve Elliott documented a 30 percent increase in business in 1991 vs. 1990. His secret for strong sales in a slow economy? Active customer relations and promotional efforts.

"We make it our job to know what our customers want and then to give it to them," Steve explains. "Having a strong identity in the community helps, too. We're a local landmark."

Vermont's Most Exciting Garden Center

Developing and maintaining a reputation as "Vermont's most exciting garden center" requires a creative, market-minded individual. Steve is just such an innovator.

One promotional highlight is the company newsletter—30,000 are stuffed into three local newspapers and an additional 4,000 are mailed to garden center customers. Elliott's newsletter is a two-color, tabloid-size piece with artwork by Chris Schlegel, who is also the grower.

The newsletter features growing tips, garden design hints, a garden center calendar of events and seasonal specials. Steve also includes a personal letter highlighting news from the business or special events.

Two-minute radio spots every morning promote what's happening in the greenhouses, and a spring customer appreciation day marks the end of the bedding plant season. Summer Country Garden Days are another big hit with customers, featuring perennial promotions.

Bus Trip a Tradition

One of Elliott's most noteworthy events, though, is filling the contract with the Balsam's Grand Resort Hotel in Dixville Notch, New Hampshire, site of the first open poll in the presidential primary. "We supply about 17,000 4-inch annuals and garden designs for the resort," Steve says, "along with 18-inch New Guinea baskets."

Steve started a tradition in 1990 when he chartered a bus and took customers to the resort for a tour of the grounds and lunch. "It's great public relations," he explains. "People get to see what types of designs and services we can offer on a bigger scale. Besides that, it's a great chance to interact with the customers."

Where does Steve come up with the ideas behind his business promotions? "It's all brainstorming. I hate being up in the office, so when I'm on the floor or in the greenhouses I'm talking over ideas with my employees. It works!"

Metro Toronto: Boom Town for Bedding [16]

by C. Anne Whealy

Barry Benjamin, manager, Cullen Country Barns, Markham, Ontario, says, "Industry-wide, I don't think we charge enough for our product, and I don't think that we pay our people well enough. We need to realize that our products have more value. If we can't get labor because we can't pay enough, then we aren't charging enough to generate sufficient profit to pay our people.

"Everyone says that they can't get more than that—well, maybe they never asked for more. If you define your market, sell and promote your quality, then you don't have to worry about price.

"Some customers will come in here and say that my competitors have packs at $1.19 (99 cents U.S.). I tell them that's fine, if the quality's the same, that's where they are going to have to buy their plants. Sometimes they come back the very same day.

"We price according to what we feel we can get for the product, and what the competition will do. Our catalog lets us lead the way, and I'm sure there's not many who will charge more than we do. If we go up, others follow suit."

Grow to Know the World [17]
by Julie A. Martens

Recognizing the United Nations' International Year of Peace in 1986, Alice Doyle and Greg Lee, Log House Plants, Cottage Grove, Oregon, brought the world to their wholesale customers and home gardeners by tracking plant origins. Some 450 plant groups and thousands of index cards later, Alice and Greg had the basis for their "Grow to Know the World" map developed by a local graphic designer.

"This project isn't a gimmick to sell more plants," Alice stresses. "We founded it on the strong need to do something to encourage people to expand their world view." The map—distributed to independent garden centers that Log House wholesales to in Oregon and Washington—highlights origins of both common and not-so-common plants.

Garden centers promote knowing plant origins as a way to know what kinds of growing conditions plants need. On the map, gardeners can look up origins of annuals, perennials, herbs and vegetables.

Showing Customers How to Use Plants

Log House Plants has organized unusual plant material into plant categories to help customers stage displays with impact. The annual flower novelties category, which includes more than 200 varieties not usually available commercially, has subgroups of dryable, cut and rockery flowers. Other categories include trailing perennial accents, annual vines and screens and blue ribbon vegetable varieties. Each category has its own full accompaniment of colorful labels and informative brochures.

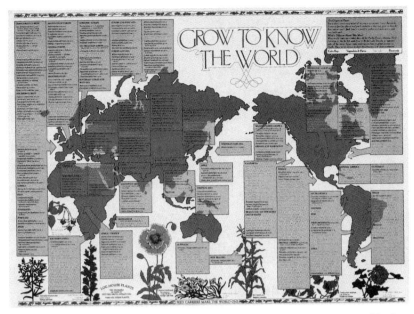

FIGURE 15. *This "Grow to Know the World" map highlights the origins of both common and uncommon plants around the world. It was a project of Log House Plants, Cottage Grove, Oregon.*

Demonstrating plant use and clear labeling is important at Log House Plants. A 50-page *Perennial Flower Manual* shows gardeners how to keep flower beds in continuous bloom. "We want to encourage people to design color displays and gardens with bloom time in mind," Alice explains.

Every perennial sold at Log House has an extra color-coded label—colors indicate time of year for flowering in Oregon. Labels also include plant light needs. The system makes for easy information transfer between retail garden centers and customers.

Log House Plants specializes in quality plant production and consumer education. All their products are gardener-friendly, developed with the customer in mind.

"We notice that gardeners are often far ahead of the growers," Alice says. "In fact, a lot of our innovations have sprouted in our own garden because of a need we discovered with our hands full of soil."

For more information about Log House Plants, "Grow to Know the World Maps" ($12 postpaid) or the *Perennial Flower Manual* contact

Log House Plants/The Bookmine,
702 Main Street,
Cottage Grove, Oregon 97424
(503) 942-2288.

Build Community Relationships [18]

by Russell Miller

In addition to one-on-one customer service provided by the staff of Bernardin's Florist, Garden Center & Landscaping, a 32,000-square-foot operation in Mokena, Illinois, there are about 15 to 20 information pamphlets and handouts at the front retail counter for customers to take home. Bernardin's also prints its own information book filled with gardening information.

One spring Bernardin's took four boxes of fiber half-flats found in the attic, filled them with 36 plants each and sold them for $3.75—as long as a customer also bought $5 of hard goods. "We called it 'Grandpa's Old-Fashioned Flat Sale,' a 20-year price roll-back," says Cathy Sanchez, greenhouse manager.

They also promoted "The Child's Garden," 15 easy-to-grow and care-for vegetables and flowering plants in a fiber flat that sold for $5.95. In the fall, children, using a coupon given with the flat, could come back and receive a free pumpkin.

Throughout the year, Cathy gives over a dozen tours of Bernardin's for school children and Master Gardeners. "Children are our future customers," Cathy says. "We educate them. Hopefully, someday, they'll be repeat customers for us. Growing plants can teach children patience, responsibility, respect for living things and a sense of accomplishment."

Pesticides and Recycling

One recent spring Cathy used plastic florist containers to display live specimens of cicadas and tent caterpillars on the front counter. "The response from the customers is very interesting," Rick Bernadin says. "Some walk by, come to a dead stop at the display and say, 'That's what I have in my tree. What do I do?' It gives us another opportunity to educate a customer."

"Pesticide use by the homeowner is very important to us," Cathy says. "No one walks out of the garden center with two bottles of Diazinon, for example, or any pesticide for that matter, before they talk to me. We want every customer to know how to properly apply and use pesticides, and in many cases, we even talk customers out of using a pesticide if we think they can get by without it."

A 4-foot by 4-foot recycling bin was added recently in front of the garden center, where customers can return plastic pots and flats for recycling. "It's catching on fast," Cathy says. "We were emptying the bin about once a week at first, but now we're emptying it twice a week."

"We are doing it to create a positive community relationship," Rick adds. "We have a sign out front that says 'Join us in recycling,' and we put the message in our ads. Customers are more than willing to join in. With the price of pots and flats, it's nice to get them back. We wash and re-use most of them."

Increase Sales with Community Goodwill [19]

by Dawn Nelson

Kim and Bruce Hawks, Niche Gardens, Chapel Hill, North Carolina, grow and sell wildflowers, perennials, shrubs and trees through a mail-order business called Niche Gardens. Working to educate both customers and employees, Kim says she finds it disturbing that people outside the industry too often perceive growers as non-professional. She wants everyone on her team to be able to answer customers' questions.

Kim extends this training process to the public. Several times a year Niche Gardens offers workshops. Recent topics include "How to Build a Rock Wall," "Designing Your Own Garden" and "Unusual Flower Arrangements."

Preserving Our Planet and Heritage

A big believer in education, Kim works with the North Carolina State Museum of Natural Sciences creating wild plant habitats on 10 different campuses across the state. This allows students to take a "hands on" approach to studying natural science. "Our program gives children an opportunity to be close to nature, which is less of a reality today than it was for their parents," she says.

Kim selects suitable species for these unique projects that boast butterfly and bird gardens along with maintained meadows on school properties. "I feel that if we can increase awareness and appreciation for the natural world, we can preserve both our planet and our heritage," she says.

An active participant in community affairs, Niche Gardens interacts with neighboring school districts by donating materials for a summer garden that is planted with flowers, vegetables and herbs to teach how earlier generations used plants.

She welcomes various garden clubs and conservation groups to tour Niche Gardens. Her motivation for doing these things is simple. "Gardening is a lifestyle for me; I can't imagine not doing this."

Niche Notes

Niche Gardens also publishes a newsletter appropriately titled *Niche Notes* in which Kim and Bruce share gardening tips, stories, product information and some news features.

Because they grow the atypical, Kim says she feels even more of a need to share information. "I view it as good advertising. Plants seen in public places become popular," she says. Do the benefits outweigh the costs of these efforts? "Absolutely," she says. "It improves people's health and lifestyle, and you can't put a price on that."

MARKETING THEORY

Marketing—What It Is and How to Do It [20]

by Ivan C. Smith

Many growers I know don't consider their organizations strong in marketing. Most have an inadequate understanding of what marketing is; the whole idea of marketing carries with it a somewhat negative connotation. Growers don't seem to appreciate the importance of effective marketing or understand how to achieve it.

I hope after you've read this article, you'll decide it's worth your while to strengthen your company's marketing capability, and you'll have a clear idea of how to go about it. A second goal is that your view of marketing will become a more positive one. Unless that happens, it's unlikely you'll commit to improved marketing.

Grasp the Marketing Concept

Let's think for a moment about something called the "marketing concept." It's a phrase coined in the 1950s by Harvard's Theodore Levitt and has regained popularity in the last couple of years as "customer satisfaction."

The marketing concept simply says that a commercial organization's chief purpose is to fulfill customer needs and solve customer problems. All an organization's decisions should be made from the viewpoint of their impact on the firm's customer serving ability.

The marketing concept acknowledges that profitability results from providing customers with value they're willing to pay for and providing that value efficiently.

ELEMENT ONE: Marketplace Intelligence

The foundation of effective marketing is the **Marketplace Intelligence System**—knowing all you possibly can about your customers and, if you don't sell directly to your product's consumers, their customers. (Don't assume **your** customers have adequate information about **their** customers. They probably don't. And, even if they do, they may be unwilling to share it with you.) It also means understanding your competition and being aware of other key marketplace factors.

- **If you sell to wholesalers or retailers, understand their business as well as you can.** Learn how they measure financial performance. Develop balance sheets and operating statements for typical and not-so-typical customers. Study them. Learn their key elements, their major leverage points.

- **Is shrinkage a critical factor in your customers' minds?** If so, what role can your organization play? Can you help your retail customers reduce shrink? If you can help them achieve, for instance, 25 percent reduction in shrinkage, it could reward you with higher prices or increases in unit volume.

- **Do your customers need additional product information** for their own use or for their customers? How important is it to them? Should you be providing it for them?

- **Does the product you ship decline in value** because of delays and inadequate handling from your location to the display floor? If you provided store-door delivery, would that be added value in your customers' eyes?

In this vital foundation category you can begin to improve your organization's marketing with a limited investment. Draw up a list of required customer information from your marketing people or sales people. Then ask yourself how much of it you do or don't already have.

If you're typical, you already know a great deal about your customers. Chances are, however, you've never systematically collected, organized and analyzed all the information. If that's the case, it probably exists in a highly fragmented form throughout your organization.

Understand Your Competition

You will notice I emphasized the need for information about competition. In one important way, your whole business goal is to outperform competition in the customers' eyes. Fortunately, you don't have to be perfect, though it's an ideal to strive for. But you do have to be superior to your competition. That's what gets you the business instead of them.

You have to understand your competition, and you have to understand them the way your customers do. Even if you seem to be "drinking from a hydrant" in a growth market with enough business for everyone, that won't last forever.

What about the "other" market arena variables I mentioned? It's helpful to organize them under these headings:

- technological

- economic

- societal

- governmental/legislative/regulatory

- natural

The goal is to identify significant factors in each of the areas, factors that have an impact on the way you run your business and factors that you act upon to strengthen your position relative to competition.

Harness Change

Here's one current example in the technological category. Today, great strides are being made in electronic inventory management. Technology promises to maximize both inventory turns and promotional effectiveness. I've heard frequently, however, that electronic inventory management won't affect floral in supermarkets because floral is a tiny percentage of retail sales and because of existing system limitations.

This is a limited perspective. True, there are "capacity" limitations now, but as retailers continue to discover the electronic inventory management's operating and marketing power, they'll want it for all product lines, and systems will be modified to make it possible. It's only a matter of time and not much time at that.

The question to explore is what you need to do to capitalize on the coming changes. Take an aggressive, pro-active stand and harness change to your competitive advantage.

ELEMENT TWO: Market Offerings

The second step in effective marketing, **Market Offerings Development/ Modification,** is often glossed over. Marketers tend to go directly to the third stage, promotion, without paying adequate attention to this element. The tendency to skip market offerings accounts for marketing's bad name in so many people's minds—companies promote capabilities their products don't have.

In such cases, the better promotion job they do, the more people they make unhappy. You can probably think of many examples where you were convinced by a promotion to buy something, only to discover that the reality fell short of the promise.

Market Offerings Development/Modification means to make yourself as valuable to your customers as you possibly can. It addresses product quality in the important but narrow sense of the word. But it has a much broader scope, incorporating all possible elements of customer-perceived value.

Often, enhancing customer value opportunities lies outside the product quality category. It may pertain to delivery, the right product mix, ease of ordering, and ready availability of order status information.

Create Constructive Change

What we're really talking about here is creating change in your organization: constructive, positive change in response to what customers consider important and what is happening and likely to happen in the marketplace.

As you get a fix on what customers are thinking about you and your competitors, get your marketing and production people and your grower together to discuss what you're learning and to think strategically about your response. If your firm practices strategic planning, here's where it fits into your overall scheme.

The president or general manager of your business sets up the needed discussions. Your marketing manager facilitates them. But it must be a management team effort. If you don't have a formal marketing function, your general manager or president can wear that hat also in the process.

In one recent case, a floral products marketer learned his customers desired a faster small order turnaround. The firm's management team discussed this, and now the company is acting to achieve the desired results.

ELEMENT THREE: Promotion

Marketing Communications/Promotion is what most people equate with marketing. But, as we've seen, there are two important steps to take before we're ready to look at promotional efforts. Assuming you've made a commitment to marketplace intelligence and to strengthening your market offering, how refreshing it will be for you to have something truly distinctive to promote.

There are 11 major promotional techniques available. Select the most appropriate mix for your situation; it's unlikely you'll use them all. You'll also want to be consistent in your promotional message and well-coordinated in different techniques.

Consistency Counts

For example, if you think media advertising is appropriate and there are publications available to reach your target market, you'll want to coordinate your advertising content with publicity releases or articles you develop. A new product or expanded service featured in your advertising can also be used in publicity releases and articles.

Publicity is, generally speaking, an underutilized promotional tool. You don't need earth-shattering news to generate good publicity. What you do need is a consistent effort, working closely with target publications' editors and making sure your material conforms to editorial requirements.

It's vital to establish clear objectives for marketing communications.

- First: Target your audience in a rifled manner.

- Second: Select promotional techniques and identify media to help you reach your target.

If the group is quite small, for example, numbering in the hundreds, you might look at direct mail and pro-active telephoning. For a larger audience you would focus more on approaches like media advertising.

AIDA

There's an old formula in marketing communications known as AIDA that stands for **Awareness, Interest, Desire, Action.** In recent years, it's been replaced by acronyms with five or six letters that simply subdivide one or two of the AIDA factors. But AIDA is still a good model.

Simply stated, you must achieve awareness before you can develop interest. Interest is a prerequisite for desire, and there won't be any action without desire.

One last factor in your promotional effort is the trade-off between reach and frequency. Assuming you don't have unlimited marketing communications dollars available, you usually have to decide between reaching a larger group of people (reach) and reaching a smaller group more often (frequency).

Possibly more marketing communications errors occur here than in any other area. Though it's possible for a marketer to repeat his message too often, I've never witnessed it.

The more common error is a failure to repeat the message enough times. A message not repeated enough is essentially wasted money. Seek expert marketing communications counsel to avoid this error.

ELEMENT FOUR: Current Business Management

Ironically, many companies fall down on the fourth step: **Current Business Management.** To me, it seems like the most basic business failure is not handling current orders well. After all, we're in business to serve customers satisfactorily. A customer order is our chance either to perform to or beyond the customer's expectations—or to fail.

I don't mean to imply that providing exactly what customers want when they want it is easy. Actually, it's quite difficult. You need an excellent forecasting system and very close cooperation and coordination between marketing and operations—a condition that exists in very few companies. My point is that current business management is very important and very basic, and is worthy of your attention.

Factors to consider are:

- How easy are you to reach?

- How easy is it to transmit orders to you?

- Are you equipped to receive orders by fax if some of your customers prefer that?

- Is it easy for customers to complete orders?

- Do you enter orders with zero errors?

- How well do you handle order inquiries?

- Have you the best possible shipping arrangements or is shipping more an afterthought?

- How about packaging?

- Is it suitable?

- Is it what customers said they wanted and needed?

ELEMENT FIVE: Continuous Customer Relationships

Finally we come to the last step: **Continuous Customer Relationships.** Many companies are realizing that supplier relationships can limit their efforts to serve their own customers better. As a result, they are reducing their supplier number and working much more closely with those they keep. Viewed from your perspective, the mirror image of this is customer relationships.

Ask yourself: Does our company regularly communicate with our customers other than to generate short-term orders? If you're not completely comfortable with your answer, you probably need to strengthen customer relationships.

Serving Customers Better

You may notice that many questions raised in conjunction with Element 1, Marketplace Intelligence System, apply here also. Understanding your customers' businesses in depth leads to good customer relationships.

Does your management team conduct joint planning discussions with your counterparts in leading customer companies? Try it. You'll find it brings you closer together and opens up new ways to better serve customers.

Electronic Data Interchange, where customers place orders directly into your order management system, is one example of relationship marketing. If it's appropriate, investigate it with selected customers. Long-term contractual relationships may be another relationship mechanism to consider.

Commit Yourself to Marketing

We've covered a lot of ground, I realize. Assuming you've decided to strengthen your marketing effort, what should you do now? Without question, the first step is to make a commitment to achieve an improved, in-depth understanding of your customers' perceptions and needs.

Then take a fresh look at your strategic planning process. Call your management team together and discuss what you're learning. Achieve consensus on a handful of market offering modifications and commit to making them.

Should you modify your promotional effort? Yes, but strengthen your market offering first. Then promote the change in the marketplace.

Five elements of successful marketing**

Continuous customer relationships

Current business management

Promotion (marketing communications)

Market offerings (development/modification)

Marketplace intelligence system

Marketing communications tools

Direct mail

Field sales

Literature

Media advertising

Packaging

Point of purchase

Pro-active telephoning

Product identification

Publicity

Sales promotions

Word of mouth

** View these elements of effective marketing form bottom to top.

NICHE MARKETING

Practical Ways to Discover and Serve Your Niche Market [21]

by Steven and Suz Trusty

Whether you are planning it or not, niche marketing is happening to your business. The components that make up your niche—products, facilities, services, prices and positioning—must fit together just so. When they do, customer loyalty is the result.

You get a feeling, an overall sensation, about a business by spending a little time there, by shopping in a retail outlet, or sitting in the office while a wholesaler pulls your order. The company's basic business concepts come through, loud and clear. If the items you want are available and the sensation you get is a pleasant one, you'll probably go back. If you feel uncomfortable, you won't return.

What Is Niche Marketing?

Everyone has a favorite grocery store. It's the one you visit the most; where you know your way around. They have the cuts of meat you like, or a super produce department, the best fresh fish or hot French bread. You know they stock the brands you want. You can count on them to have the cake you ordered, ready as promised.

The shelves, floors and carts are always clean. The fellow at the service desk calls you by name. The checkers all know your face; you never have to show identification on your checks. You know the ropes of carry-out or drive-up procedure.

Suppose you're headed home and need to pick up milk or a loaf of bread. You pop into the closest supermarket, not your regular store. How do you feel? A bit strange, a little wary, rather critical?

Both of these stores offer a complete line of grocery and home care items. Both are located within easy driving distance from your home. Yet it would take something pretty special to be able to entice you away from your familiar supermarket and your usual shopping pattern.

At some point, you develop a reliance upon your regular store to supply your needs. As your interests and eating patterns change, so do your store's offerings. The produce department expands to make room for more varieties of lettuce, fresh mushrooms and exotic fruits. A salad bar, fresh fish selections and call-ahead pizza pick-up are added. The in-store postal counter now also offers UPS services. You can drop off clothes for dry cleaning or shoes for repair.

Key to Success

That's niche marketing. Whether you are planning it or not, niche marketing is happening in your business. Everyone who walks through your door forms an opinion about your operation. The key to success in the '90s and beyond is controlling that opinion, developing your market niche.

Does that mean you're going to have to make changes? Yes and no. If you are running a profitable operation, have a base of long-standing customers, and are seeing continual growth in both areas, chances are you're doing pretty well at finding the right niche. A bit of fine tuning should keep you on line and bring in extra business.

If you've done quite well in the past, but recent years' sales have been flat, or you have registered a drop in sales or lowered profits, and you've lost several of your regular shoppers, you may be facing some big changes.

See Your Business Objectively

In either instance, the first thing you'll need to do is take a long, hard look at where you are right now. Consider how your business looks and how you think it feels to shop there. Drive in one morning and imagine you've never seen the place before.

Do you want to go in? Why? Do you know where to park, which door to enter? What do you feel like when you get inside? Are you pleased with that first glance, drawn to an interesting display, guided to specific areas? How does it smell? How does it sound?

Can you quickly and easily find the greenhouses, the outside sales yard, the checkout area? Can you identify the people who work there? Go to your desk and jot down some notes about all this, but don't form firm opinions yet.

Hear Your Customers

Then tuck your ego in your back pocket and spend some time talking with and listening to your customers. Do you expect your sales staff to guess what plants each shopper wants without talking to that shopper first? Are you trying to please your customers without finding out what they want and need?

Look at the strategy of your supermarket. They carefully consider the changing wants and needs of their customers before adding new departments. On a few of the store's busiest days, shoppers are offered tasty samples of fresh fish. A special fresh fish sale touts good prices. You try a sample or two; maybe you buy some of the specials. Others also respond positively. Soon a full selection fish department is added.

You, along with the store's other shoppers, registered your opinions by your interest in the samples offered and your willingness to buy. A store's shoppers can become special marketing consultants, a focus group on new product offerings. The input provided is extremely accurate. This input is compiled and reviewed by the store's department heads, managers and owners. The shoppers' response leads to the opening of the new department.

Other in-store product testing will show the supermarket that their customers are not sufficiently interested to warrant adding or expanding a particular line. Shoppers make decisions with their dollars.

Survey Customers and Employees

Horticultural customers are just as willing to tell us their likes and interests. Let everyone in your company know that you want their help in defining your market niche. Ask for and listen to their opinions.

Ask them to share the feedback gained from your customers by concentrating on listening to these shoppers for one week. They should carry a pencil and notepad to jot down the comments and questions during that period. Let your staff know you want to hear the good and the bad.

Have them drop their notes in a collection box daily. Read them all. Follow up on any particular hot spots or surprises by spending some time of your own in that area, interacting with customers and gaining further information.

Then meet with the entire staff at the end of the week. Make this an open meeting. Let everyone voice their comments and opinions. No one should be afraid to speak up honestly or be put down for their input. Have someone take good notes on this meeting, and review them soon afterward.

Now pull out those notes you made after your initial look at your own reactions to your company's look and feel. Compare notes. You will have compiled some basic information about the status of your operation and current customers' views.

Your market niche will be outlined by the information you gather. Remember, it's easier to fill a need than to create one. The changes you make to strengthen your niche and improve your business will be those needed to better fill your customers' needs.

Know the Whys Behind Your Business

Next examine your marketing mix components; the parts of your business operation that appeal to customers. To market your company's goods and services most efficiently, you should be able to explain why you are carrying each specific product. Each service should fill a definite need. There should be a logical sequence for each procedure. You should not only know what you are doing, but why you're doing it.

Products

- **Start with the products you carry.** The level of quality should match your customers' demands. Do shoppers want top of the line, good or just adequate? Perhaps you serve a broader base of shoppers and need to carry products ranging from the top of good to just under spectacular, or from a bit more than adequate to mid-level good.

  Is this product something your shoppers will want? Does it make their gardening experience easier or more satisfying? Does it provide real benefits?

  Imagine a few of your steady customers looking over a specific plant or bag of media. How would each react? To find out for sure, ask them.

Facilities and Services

- **Consider your facilities and services package,** the where and how of getting the products and services to your customers when they want and need them. This includes your business location, its physical layout and design, traffic in the area, parking access, hours of operation, delivery and custom services.

  Though all of these are separate elements of your business, the way they interact shapes the customers' perceptions of your company and your overall market image. You will be tied to some of these elements; others will be quite flexible. Some may seem to be unchangeable, but after considering various alternatives, can be altered or adjusted.

  Another way of looking at your facilities and services package is to consider what aspects of your company's operations make it tough for your customers to buy from you. Consider the changing lifestyles of your customers. The majority of your customers may be single parents or two-income families. Shopping from 9 to 5 during the week is impossible, and weekends are becoming increasingly hectic.

  It is fairly easy to extend your hours, set up a lighting system for your parking area, or add an additional delivery crew. A florist shop in Clearwater, Florida, added a drive-through pick-up window to better serve its customers.

  Other problems call for more complex solutions. Perhaps your location, which was once at the outskirts of town, is now the center of a residential neighborhood or is being slowly surrounded by an industrial area. Traffic may have shifted from your crossroads to a new highway nearby. The manufacturing business next door, whose parking lot you had arranged to use on weekends, will now be running Saturday shifts, completely eliminating your overflow parking.

A few ideas for solving the location problem could be to sell the existing property and move to a new site, set up satellite operations or change the focus of the business. Keep an open mind. It's been said that if you don't see a workable solution, you're not looking in the right places.

When business offices grew up around one retail greenhouse, the company started sending a weekly flyer to each office offering specials, quick noon-hour service and a program to call or fax ahead to pick up after work. Changes were made in the company's level and type of customer service.

More employees were scheduled during the office work week, the aisles of the display greenhouses were paved, paper towels were hung at the end of each bench, a fax machine was installed to receive orders, greater emphasis was placed on pre-planted containers of color and larger sizes of bedding plants. What had initially appeared to be a threat turned into a very profitable marketing strategy.

Set Appropriate Prices

- **Pricing is also a factor in your marketing niche.** This doesn't mean you have to hold prices at 1968 levels or meet the advertised specials of your chain competitors. It means that your prices must be appropriate for the products and services you offer.

   Feedback from your customers will give you a starting point to gauge this. Prices are appropriate when consumers react favorably to them. If your shoppers oh and ah over a beautiful display of plants, but leave without buying any, your prices are too high. If they scoop them all up within the hour, your prices are too low. Of course, your customers' reactions won't often be this obvious. They will range somewhere between these extremes. With a bit of practice, you can become adept at reading them.

   A basic rule of pricing is that no one will ever pay more than you ask for a product or service. It follows that it is much easier to start with a fairly high price, and lower it if need be, than to start with a low price and attempt to raise it.

   The initial price must not be high enough to be out of line for the perceived value of the product or service. It must fit within the range of what your customers would be willing to pay and what similar items would cost if sold by companies like your's. The price must be considered fair for the value received.

To set this pricing range, you need to know the pricing levels of your direct competitors and of companies with market niches similar to your own. Shop other outlets, monitor their ads, establish your own profit margin criteria and consider manufacturers' suggested pricing.

Another area to become familiar with is the relative value assigned to products in other industries that might compete with your products for your customers' dollars. It isn't sound business to set too low a value on our products. Many of our products increase in value over the years. Consider the extended life of trees and shrubs, strawberry and asparagus beds, peonies and cushion mums. Set prices along reasonable guidelines, at a level that will support your costs and make a profit and will still be considered fair by your customers.

Position

- **Your position in the marketplace** is the last component of your niche. This includes the look and style of your store fixtures, displays and signage; the skill and knowledge level of your personnel; the mix of customer education and information you provide in proportion to selling them something; and the advertising, public relations and promotions you feature.

  These factors should work together to bring about the level of sales required to allow your company to fulfill your customers' expectations profitably. Positioning allows you to appeal to the targeted group of consumers who will want what you have to offer and to get them the message that you're ready and able to provide it.

  Adjustments in this area are constant. As your customers' interests change and their knowledge in certain areas grows, you'll need to expand and grow to better serve them. The hard part here is to keep this whole area coordinated. Each segment reflects on the others.

  If you position your company as an information and education center, you must have well-qualified, communicative personnel on hand to work with the customers. You will need to provide how-to handout sheets and hold seminars and workshops.

  Point-of-purchase materials and displays must convey the merchandise's benefits, how to best use it, that it's available and how much it costs. Send an informative newsletter to all of your regular customers.

  Key your advertising and promotions to having just what your shoppers need at exactly the time they need it. Your phones must be manned by people who will cheerfully and accurately answer questions.

If your company's niche is the best source of perennials around, you will need to have the greatest selection of quality perennials in your area. Your staff should all have an excellent knowledge of varieties, growth habits, pest control, cultivation practices and possible uses.

Stock everything your customers could possibly want or need relating to perennials. Use your newsletter to alert them to potential problems, remind them of the proper times to take action, and offer them insights on growing or using their plants. Promotions should highlight and revolve around perennials.

Don't send mixed signals—define your niche very clearly. Don't advertise high quality and offer mediocre products. Don't promote great specials and fail to provide excellent value for the dollar. Don't promise quick delivery and show up late.

The components that make up your niche in the market—products, facilities and service package, prices and positioning—must all fit together like the pieces of a jigsaw puzzle. Whatever market you serve, whatever your niche, strive to fulfill your customers' expectations of what you can and will provide them. The more closely your company matches the expectations of your targeted customers, the more successful you will be.

FIGURE 16. *Determine the elements of your market niche—perhaps provide a pleasant spot devoted to customer information. Photo taken at Southern Perennial Growers, Newnan, Georgia.*

Everybody Wins with Environmental Marketing [22]

by Ann Turner Whitman

Environmental marketing isn't just about recycling. It's about promoting a healthy and sustainable way of life. We ignore the growing concern about the environment at our peril. In a poll conducted by The Consumer Network last fall, shoppers ranked the environment third on a list of concerns. Only the economy and health care ranked higher.

To profit from consumers' environmental concerns, you should target specific areas that your customers perceive as problems and sell them ways to solve those problems. Help them feel good about themselves and about you.

"People of all economic and social levels want to do their part to save the environment. They want to buy, use and have environmentally favorable products," says R.J. Hutton, chairman of the board, in his introduction to Conard-Pyle's 1991–1992 nursery catalog. "We are the ones who can satisfy these wants better than anyone else . . . we are the ones who can do more than all the others for the urban, suburban and rural landscape."

Our industry is uniquely poised to capitalize on the ground swell of environmental consciousness. Plants seem to offer all the answers to the earth's woes: wildlife habitat, water and air quality, natural beauty, climate control, as well as opportunities for natural pest control, organic and inorganic waste recycling and, above all, education.

Water Conservation and Quality

Scarce natural rainfall and diminishing aquifers make xeriscaping a necessity in many communities. Growers and retailers who cater to the demands for drought-tolerant plants find a ready market. Alan Shapiro of San Falasco's Nursery (wholesale) and The Plant Shoppe (retail) in Gainesville, Florida, report that they are growing and selling more native plants because they fit in with the xeriscaping concept and require less pest control, water, fertilizer and general maintenance.

Water quality, too, concerns consumers and growers alike. If you have changed practices to improve water conservation and quality in your business, let customers know and help them do the same. Local water departments could willing partners in seminars that promote a xeriscaping theme.

Climate Control and Wildlife Habitat

Public concern over ozone depletion and global warming has made tree planting the symbolic centerpiece of Earth Day celebrations and community group organizations nationwide. Get in on the action by sponsoring these events. But let people know that *all* green plants improve air quality and reduce ozone depletion, not just trees. Educate customers also about using plants for climate control.

Besides cleaning the air, plants provide food and shelter for birds, butterflies and animals. While that statement may be obvious, it is also a great selling point for many a budding suburban naturalist.

Offer "gardening for wildlife" and "how to attract birds and butterflies" workshops. Sell theme gardens consisting of plants that attract butterflies and hummingbirds or that produce edible fruit. Tie in related products, such as books, feeders and birdbaths.

Natural Pest Controls

The public hue and cry over pesticide use is spreading from food products to include all aspects of the plant industry. We must be prepared to take the lead on this issue. Using progressive and pro-active pest control methods and helping customers do the same will increase our profits in more ways than one.

Integrated pest management not only saves on chemical costs, but it also advertises your environmentally friendly practices and gives your business a positive image that builds customer confidence and loyalty.

Alan Shapiro at The Plant Shoppe reports that they are increasing their retail inventory of organic pest controls. He is especially intrigued with containers of ladybugs that he saw offered in another garden center. "Most everyone wants to use organic pest controls," he says.

Composting

In Vermont, take your used Christmas tree to J.S. Lang and Co. in Essex Junction, and they will give you a $4 coupon redeemable toward a purchase of $20 or more in nursery stock. They will even take your tree if you bought it from someone else.

Debbie Lang says her husband, Jonathan, thought of the idea to bring customers into their new garden center. "Everyone wins," she says. "The customer wins and we win." The Langs shred the trees for compost that they use in their nursery and landscape business.

Recycling and Reusing Plastic

Helping customers dispose of their plastic waste is another way to gain their loyalty. Bill Bettinger of Bettinger Farms, Toledo, Ohio, says, "The consumer is very aware of the recycling concept but finds it's hard to participate." To make it easier for their customers to recycle, Bettinger's places pallet bins by their wholesale production doors for recyclable plastics.

Bettinger's has a similar arrangement at their retail location. Although they don't pay for the returned plastic, their customers like the bins, Bill reports. "On rainy days," he says, "employees sort and palletize the plastic for shipment to Dick Bonnet's Plastic Recycling Services in Parkersburg, West Virginia."

Growers and retailers who do pay for returned containers also report customer satisfaction. Most growers reuse the pots instead of recycling them. Other innovative ways to dispose of plastic include grinding up styrofoam to use as a soil amendment or for drainage in the bottom of large containers.

Education

Regardless of the angle you choose to market your environmental concern, education will have to be part of the package. Consumers want to "do the right thing" and it's up to you to help them in ways that will profit your business while helping the environment. Incorporate educational information in your packaging, signage, advertising, seminars, press releases and newsletters.

Don't overlook children in your educational efforts. Kids are more environmentally aware than adults and have a tremendous impact on the buying habits of their parents. Support school curricula, cooperate with youth groups, sponsor environmental projects, include games, puzzles and environmental information with products, pursue public relations opportunities, and advertise in environmentally oriented media.

If you're already using environmentally friendly practices in your business, profit from them! Align your business image with the environmental movement, and promote your good deeds. Consider the success story of McDonald's Corporation, the fast-food giant, once much maligned and litigated against for its wasteful packaging. The company became partners with the Environmental Defense Fund, changed its packaging, and its public image. It worked for McDonald's—it can work for you.

MERCHANDISING & DISPLAY

Merchandising: the Art of Profitable Persuasion [23]

by John H. Saxtan

Even if you think your retail sales are good, chances are they could be better. And chances are you can increase sales without a lot of additional expense. The secret is in merchandising, making your products so attractive that people just can't pass up the opportunity to buy them. "Buy" is the operative word; you don't just want to make things more attractive, you want to make them more attractive to *buy*.

A visit to an upscale department store or large supermarket reveals many key merchandising techniques. Most good department stores use the services of professional display and merchandising personnel, but you don't have to go to that extreme to benefit from what they know. Supermarkets, with their bin displays, endcaps, shelf talkers and keen knowledge of moving volumes of merchandise and maximizing profits, use effective merchandising techniques. They provide examples for some of the following suggestions.

Eye to Thigh

Psychologically and physically, the prime selling "space" is the vertical range from your customers' thigh level to eye level, the area 3 to 6 feet above ground level. At your local supermarket you find that brand name products are usually on the shelves that sit between chest and eye height; lesser known brands are usually relegated to the lower shelves.

The reasoning here is obvious—what is seen first gets the customer's attention first. This means getting your flats and pots off the floor and up closer to the customer's eyes. If you sell in a greenhouse, benches are at a good height for sales appeal. If you sell outdoors or in a retail store, put flats, pots and vases of flowers on tables or carts to raise them off the floor. Varying the heights of display tables adds sales interest and appeal.

If product sizes vary, say 4-, 6-, 8-inch mums, arrange vertically, with the smaller pots high and the largest pots near or on the floor. For those who believe people want to see bedding plants displayed on the ground—

FIGURE 17. *Varying the heights of displays adds sales interest and appeal. Plus plenty of signage helps customers find what they want.*

because that's the way they will look when planted—I suggest a visit to a shoe store. Shoes are seldom displayed on the floor even though that's where they are used.

Large, heavy items like potted palms, specimen size foliage and bags of bark chips or soil, do belong on the ground, but stacking brings the top bag closer to the customer. The smaller the item the more important that it be displayed between thigh and eye levels.

Group Products by Color

Consumers are more color conscious than ever, and color sells. Group all like products (impatiens in one group, geraniums in another group, etc.) in one area and arrange by color, starting with the darkest color on the right. Reason: Most people read from left to right and their eyes follow this pattern when "reading" your products.

Arranging plants by color groups allows customers to quickly find, or discover, what they are looking for and make comparisons. Start with reds on the left, then corals, salmons, pinks, white, yellows, oranges, blues and fuchsias.

Put Your "Big Draw" at the Back

If you are having a special sale on an item, place it in the back or center of the sales area—to draw customers past other products and prompt additional sales. Leave ample room around the display so it's set off as special, and for smooth traffic flow. Call attention to the sale items with large signs over the display and with signs directing customers to the special.

Keep Displays Full

It's human nature—nobody likes to buy the last of anything. People assume that a less than full display has been picked over and what's left is less than the best, no matter how good it really is.

Replenish displays with additional goods as often as possible to keep them looking full. If stock is running low, arrange what is left in one or more compact groups to create a fuller display. When only a few items remain, reduce the display size or move to a smaller area. Fill in the emptied area with different product.

Create a Pleasant Environment

Neatness counts no matter how large or small your sales area. The basics of a pleasant environment call for a clean, well-lighted place, but there are numerous selling opportunities beyond that. Are aisles wide enough for easy movement? People don't like to touch or be touched by others when shopping.

Lighting dramatically affects an indoor sales area. Spotlights call attention to displays and signs. Good lighting lets customers see what they are buying; poor lighting may not only distort colors, but may also give the impression that an area isn't as clean as it could be.

Indoors, vary light intensity with different types of lighting and spotlights. Aisles and walkways do not need as bright a light as signs and products. If the lighting is evenly bright throughout a store, there is little opportunity to spotlight and call attention to products.

Stimulate the senses of smell and hearing, and you add to the environment. Pleasant, upbeat or holiday music creates a relaxed shopping atmosphere. Simmer potpourri at Christmas or perfume the air in spring and summer with flower accents.

The smell of fresh pumpkin pie or spiced apple cider (possible customer giveaways on fall weekends) can keep customers from rushing out too quickly. Encourage them to linger and buy. Giveaways, such as coffee and cookies, carry no obligation, but customers often feel slightly obligated and motivated to buy something.

Add Value (and Profit) to Products

When adding value to a product, you can charge more than what you added. Putting foil and a ribbon on a pot plant for Mother's Day adds value, and customers will gladly pay more for the added appearance and convenience of a dressed gift.

Tie on a fancy ribbon and add a helium balloon to packs, flats, or pots, and add a pick that says "Happy Easter" or "Happy Birthday." If the added cost to you is $1, charge $2 to $3 more for the item. You'll be surprised how many sell.

A wicker basket attractively planted with small foliage plants commands a higher price than selling the items individually. You can also display items together, but price them separately. A pot plant displayed in an attractive basket or container often leads to a combined sale even though the items are not priced as a set.

Use Signs to Sell, Inform

According to an American Floral Marketing Council survey, customers often hesitate to buy if an item is not clearly identified by name. Rather than ask, they will choose to buy something else or nothing at all. Clearly label all items as to name, characteristics and cultural information.

Unpriced merchandise is also annoying to customers. The general reaction is to assume too high or too low a price. Rather than ask the price, many customers will simply avoid embarrassment and choose not to buy.

Sales area directional and identity signs let customers find what they want quickly. Signs should be neat, simple and easy to read. Large signs, high in the air over the appropriate areas, should identify where annuals, perennials, hanging baskets, foliage plants, etc. can be found.

Signs are doubly important if you often redesign your sales area. Customers familiar with one layout can rely on signs to direct them to new locations.

For specials and sales items, a large blackboard placed at the entrance to the store or sales area can be used effectively. A blackboard's non-permanent appearance lends a flavor of something really special that may not be around or on sale very long.

Clearly mark sale items to promote buying and avoid confusion.

Add-on Sales

Promote sales of accessory items by displaying them next to prime sellers. For example, group pots next to potting soil. You will sell more African violet food if it's displayed next to the African violets. Even if you have a separate display or area for things such as plant food, soil, pots and macrame hanging basket holders, display some of these next to the products or plants for which they will be used.

Bundling products, or creating a kit is another way to add to sales. Combination pots are a good example. Display one or more made-up combination pots, and sell the necessary materials next to the display. List the materials used for each pot on a sign, and next to that display everything needed to achieve the same look—plants, soil, pots, plant food, watering cans.

Sales of product can be doubled or tripled by pricing them "two for" and "three for." This works especially well on small items (plant food, pots, small plants) that might normally be purchased individually.

It also works well on products that are normally sold in multiples, such as packs, but will stimulate buying in groups of two, four, six or three, six, nine, instead of lesser multiples. This adds incremental sales. Be prepared to sell these items singly when requested, but you can charge more for a single than its fractional unit price.

Demonstrate Products

Whenever possible, show products as they would be used. Plant up or arrange products to look like small patches of garden. Show color combinations such as a bed of yellow marigolds edged with blue ageratum, or pink geraniums and silvery dusty miller.

Make Products Accessible

If you make people work to get your product, many won't bother. You might be surprised how many times a customer will not buy something because they couldn't reach it. If your display is more than an arm's reach to the center, change it or plan on not selling what's in the middle. This also applies to products displayed too high, like hanging baskets. Place hanging baskets close to eye level, so they can be easily taken down.

Sell High to Low

If a customer asks, "Do you have large foliage plants? I want something for my living room," start by mentioning or showing your highest priced plants, then work your way down. If you start high, every time you mention a lower price, you're lowering the customer's price resistance. Going from high to low will often result in a sale at a higher price than if you work from low to high.

Convenience

Convenience covers many factors that make customers favor one store over another. Among the major conveniences customers favor are store hours (open early, open late), acceptance of major credit cards and personal checks, ample parking and having enough sales personnel who know the store and its products.

A major inconvenience at busy times is long waiting lines at checkout counters. At peak sales periods one employee can speed the process by writing up sales slips for customers waiting in line before they reach the cashier.

Provide shopping carts, wagons or dollies to hold customers' purchases. If the carts are too small, you may discourage additional purchases. Large carts (within limits) are not only more convenient for customers to use, but can actually stimulate additional sales.

Some customers want delivery. This can be handled by charging for the delivery or offering delivery only on certain items or purchases over a certain dollar amount.

Accepting phone orders, helping with garden planning, planting trees and shrubs are conveniences that can be offered and charged for.

Let Common Sense Prevail

Many merchandising techniques are based on common sense. Put yourself in the customer's place and ask, "What would make me want to buy?" As an owner/manager ask yourself, "What can I do to make people buy more?" When you are a customer, observe what other merchants do to make their products more appealing, more attractive to buy.

There are many sophisticated techniques to merchandising, but you don't have to become a specialist in order to profit from the basics. Observe the persuasion techniques major merchandisers use. It's not a capital offense to steal a good sales idea—it's smart business.

What Color Are Your Sales?[24]

by John H. Saxtan

For a long time now, horticultural marketers have talked about selling plants when they are in color. We have heard that "color sells" and that consumers want "instant color" for their gardens and homes. This isn't new, but what may be news to you is that the color of the packaging, the store decor or selling environment, your logo and the clothing your workers wear can have a strong influence on how your products are perceived.

Color is **very** important when it comes to selling; in fact, according to at least one color expert, color accounts for 60 percent of a consumer's buying decision. That means that if you have the right colors or can use colors to influence a sale, your selling job is already more than half completed for you. That's how important color is. The other 40 percent of the sale is based on the traditional sales features of convenience, price, size, etc.

A look at the major colors and how people react to them, plus how they are commonly used, can aid you in increasing your sales and customer satisfaction.

It All Starts With Red

Red has many meanings for us. It means fire, it means heat, it commands our attention. Red vies with yellow for being the fastest color we see. Red actually causes physiological changes in our bodies. Our blood pressure increases, our heart beats faster, breathing increases, and more adrenalin is released into our system. We literally get excited around red.

How can you use red? Red flowers and red objects will always be popular. Since men prefer yellow-based reds and women prefer blue-based reds, this may influence which reds sell better depending on whether you have more men or women shopping.

Use red to call attention to things. Red signs or red lettering command attention. Paint display tables red to call attention to items, or paint your delivery truck red it you want to build awareness of your business. Dress your employees in red if you want customers to be able find them quickly.

Popular Blue

When people are asked what their favorite color is, the overwhelming answer is usually blue. Blue is a very calming color. Like red, blue actually affects our physical reactions, but they are just the opposite of red. Blue lowers the blood pressure and slows the heart.

How can you use blue? Blue in a logo can reflect competence. Dark blues can be used to convey authority.

Blue is a recessive color. If you want to make a garden end or some part of your store look further away, put blue there. Blue flowers don't advance the way red ones do, they increase the perceived distance.

Fast Yellow

Bright, cheerful yellow is reportedly the fastest color we see. Yellow is also associated with quickness and being inexpensive. Things that are yellow are often new and exciting—many spring flowers are yellow.

How can you use yellow? In merchandising, yellow is a good "sale" color. It says fast and cheap. Color a table yellow, and put sale items on it. Use yellow cardboard to feature special prices. Have employees wear yellow to be found quickly in a store. Because yellow is a highly visible "fast" color, painting your delivery van yellow can gain you visibility and say "fast delivery" to customers.

Yellow in a garden will capture the eye quicker, so it is a good color around fountains or special features in a garden. Around steps or other hazards, yellow flowers can act as a subtle warning.

Yellow is a good mixer. Put yellow with a deep blue, and the combination will appeal to more people than blue alone. The same is true of yellow with dark greens. When yellow combines with the vitality of red, it becomes even more vital and exciting.

Restful Green

It's probably no surprise that green is the most restful color to the eyes. It's also the color of life, as in horticulture, where green means new and growing.

FIGURE 18. *Yellow flowers are eye-catchers and work well in combination with other colors. Photo by American Takii Inc., Salinas, California.*

How can you use green? Even though green is so closely associated with florists, growers and interiorscapers, it may not be the best color to use in promoting your business. Studies have shown that we don't take green seriously in business. If you aren't closing sales or getting paid what you asked, could it be the green?

Don't abandon green, just use it carefully.

Affordable Orange

Orange is usually associated with fall. Leaves turn orange, and orange mums and other flowers are then in demand. Just as fall is a transition from the heat of summer to the cool of winter, orange is a transitional color. It says "affordable" and "middle of the road."

How can you use orange? If you use dark green a lot in your signage, you may be appealing to only 5 percent or less of the population. By combining that green with orange you can open that appeal to a much greater number. Aside from its association with fall, orange is a good color to say "affordable" in your store.

Formal Black and White

Black and white go together because they are such natural opposites, and also because they are often used and thought of in conjunction with each other.

How can you use black and white? Use them to convey authority, or combine black and white for a very formal look. A black and white tile floor in the wedding area of a florist shop will lend formality and authority, while black and white uniforms for employees will lend to an authoritative image.

Creative Grey

While grey is not really one of the major color groups, it is currently becoming THE new neutral. Grey is gradually replacing beige in interiors and exteriors as a decorating style.

It is an ideal color for work areas where you want to encourage creativity. It is restful, it is neutral, it is non-intrusive. Grey clothing conveys a "friendly authority" image, and therefore is excellent in business.

Color Consciousness

Becoming a color expert, or at least as expert as you need to be for your business, isn't all that difficult. Visit clothing stores to find out what colors are popular. For interior trends, talk to an interior decorator or to the sales manager of a paint store in your town. Become aware of color as you move through the world.

Successful Color Combinations [25]

by Ann Turner Whitman

"At the point of purchase, color is the single most important thing. It's more important than price or design. It's easier to sell a customer a different product than they wanted if it's in the right color," says Kenneth Charbonneau, color and merchandising manager for Benjamin Moore & Co. paints and past-president of the international Color Marketing Group.

At *GrowerExpo '92,* Ken Charbonneau invited members of the floral trade to step out of their industry and into his, to learn something from color stylists and then relate that knowledge to their own industry. "The fashion industry used to set the color trends, but now all industries are contributing to color directions, including the floral industry," Charbonneau reported.

Growers are ready to listen. Goldsmith Seeds, Gilroy, California, focused their 1992 pack trials on color and hired Ken as a consultant. Under his direction, Goldsmith replicated a house facade three times using different paint and landscaped with color-coordinated bedding plants. Trial beds were also by color.

Using and promoting popular colors and color combinations can significantly increase your sales. "Think of yourselves as a major accessory in any space. The most specified thing by interior designers in rooms today is flowers and foliage," Ken declares. " *The most!*" Consumers want flowers to complement their homes both inside and out.

Predicting Color Trends

Color trends "are an evolution, not a revolution," Ken notes. "Colors ease in, take over, reach a peak, and then go down in popularity. When looking for a trend, start at the top—the expensive, high-end products—then the medium to higher priced. By the time it has filtered down to the lowest priced products, the trend is over." The current life cycle of popular colors is about five to six years.

Popular colors usually reflect world events. "Movements within any period have a strong influence," Ken explains. "The bicentennial made a big impact on color and color directions."

Today's color trends show new preoccupations. When the economy slows down and times get tough, people get more conservative and want their choices to be more careful. "Classic colors, such as navy and indigo, become more popular, especially in tough times," Ken says.

Environmental awareness has also brought earth-related colors and garden greens into fashion, while the re-emergence of Russia and Eastern Europe has heralded a return of rich, old-world colors, such as purple and gold. Even the Gulf War had a significant impact by bringing khaki and olive-browns to the fashion forefront.

Ken also sees several major directions emerging in color uses: color layering and combinations that give the viewer a sense of detail, the increasing use of texture, sheen and pattern in the absence of color, and a return to clearer, cleaner colors. By color group, here are his predictions for the next two years.

Blue

"Blue is the No. 1 corporate identity because it connotes stability, longevity," especially classics like navy, Ken reports. The blues are evolving into clearer, cleaner colors like periwinkle, sapphire, cobalt, porcelain and China blue. These bright blues are best used as accent colors and in combinations with white and bright, new yellows.

Purple, Violet

Because "grey is the No.1 neutral of the decade, purples and violets have a good chance of emerging and being utilized right now," Ken says. For a successful combination, use red-violet with its opposite on the color wheel, yellow-green.

Pink, Rose, Mauve

Mauve is decreasing in importance, but will still be a mass-market color for several more years. This color family is also becoming cleaner and clearer, evolving into pink and magenta. "If I had to give you a direction for this color group, it would be pink," Ken states. "I was glad to hear the emphasis in geranium production on all the new pink varieties. Pink is extremely important in both interior and exterior."

Red

Another classic color group, red, including deep wine, garnet and the berry shades, remains popular. Ken warns, however, that red is the "most regional of colors. What's good for New England and the snowbelt isn't appropriate for southern California," although smaller doses can be adapted to warmer climates. What's new in this group is red-orange and even orange, though orange isn't likely to become popular on the West Coast, Ken thinks.

Coral, Shrimp, Peach

"If you want to put some bucks into a color direction, it's peach evolving into the coral shades," Ken predicts. "We see a return to orange; not the bright oranges, but the coral ones and the deepened red ones." Coral combines well with the "new" greens.

Earth-Related Colors

Earth-related colors are an extension of the coral family. Dusty pink, peach, rosy stucco, orange, tobacco brown, orange-gold, paprika, cinnamon and Indian curry colors are popular, especially balanced with blues and weathered blues. The classics—terra cotta and brick red—remain important.

Yellow, Gold, Curry

"Yellow has never been a big volume color, but it's an important accent color. Also, psychologically we **need** daffodils in February," Ken states. The trend here is toward golden browns, Indian spice tones and marigold colors.

Turquoise, Jade, Green

Good news for growers: Ken reports that "garden greens" reminiscent of English cottage gardens and conservatories are popular, especially combined with coral and rose. Turquoise and jade green are becoming very important. "If I had to bank something on the future, it would be turquoise," he predicts.

Neutrals, Pales, Pastels

An important new color group consists of white tinted very subtly with pale hints of other popular colors, such as periwinkle, peach, coral, violet or green. These pale colors balance the deeper colors that are emerging. The key to these colors is using white as a foil to emphasize the subtle shades.

Warm-based whites, such as creamy off-white, linen and oriental silk are popular now. Essential in combinations, neutrals are the perfect complement for strong, vibrant colors as well as the new paler shades. The new neutrals are peach and rose.

Regional Preferences

When predicting what colors will be popular, consider regional preferences. Income level, type of community and ethnic background dictate color choices as does terrain, season, light quality and climate. Dark colors that sell in the snowbelt may be unsuitable for southern markets, for example. Pastels and subtler colors appeal to the South, West Coast and upscale markets, while bright rose, violets and burgundy are more popular in the North and middle-income brackets.

Ken talked about "pockets of specialty," where color selections respect the region's special light and unique geographical conditions. Hawaii's tropical climate, for example demands bright, rich colors that reflect the islands' lush flora. Mauve and grey would be inappropriate, according to Ken.

Custom Blend Your Seed

Proprietary seed mixes are one way to satisfy your particular market while distinguishing your business from the competition's. Seed companies blend bedding plant varieties to suit regional and seasonal preferences.

Express Seed Company, Oberlin, Ohio, for example, offers blends such as Pansy Pastel Mix, Pansy Intensity Mix and Pansy Blue, Pink or Rainbow Mixes. The Pansy Pastel Mix contains Imperial Pink Shades, Maxim Marina, Crown White, Cream Crown and Crystal Bowl Primrose. This blend is popular in the South for fall and winter sales. Express and other companies offer similar mixes for other bedding plants and will make custom blends to your specifications.

Marketing Color Is Key

Ken recommends that retailers become color consultants for their customers. A tremendous market exists for custom-designed window boxes and planters and color-coordinated landscapes. Consumers want their flowers to match their decor. "They just don't know where to start," Ken says. "They want suggestions and examples."

When doing exterior design, curb appeal becomes very important. "What industry can contribute more to curb appeal than this one?" he asks.

Ken suggests using color swatches or paint chips of the existing exterior house and trim colors when picking out bedding and nursery plants. Also be aware of the colors of the roof and natural materials around the building, as well as those of neighboring sites. Try to create a sense of detail in the landscape using color combinations.

He stresses the importance of before and after photographs and keeping a portfolio to show potential customers. Make up store displays using paint chips, photographs and color-coordinated bedding plants. Use magazine photos if you don't have your own.

He suggests merchandising plants by color groups instead of species or putting complementary colors next to each other to give customers ideas. Emphasize new colors and varieties through special signage or displays.

Tradition Is In

Trends in exterior colors tend to be more conservative and historical than interior and fashion colors. A wave of "traditionalism" is sweeping the country, bringing with it period-style houses and landscapes. English cottage gardens, Colonial kitchen gardens and Victorian cutting gardens are in demand to satisfy consumers' new interest in tradition.

Growers and retailers who want to satisfy their customers and increase their sales will take color trends and marketing very seriously. We are in the business of selling color; let's use it to our advantage.

Designing eye-catching bowls, baskets and beds is easy if you follow a few simple rules. Use a color wheel if you need a place to start. Possible plant combinations are nearly endless. These suggestions will get you started.

- **Opposites attract.** Colors that are opposite one another on the color wheel look good together. Try orange New Guinea impatiens with Vinca minor (periwinkle); purple lisianthus or petunias with yellow petunias or zinnias; copper snapdragons with blue saliva; violet-red impatiens with pale green hostas.

- **Safety in numbers.** Three colors that are equidistant on the color wheel make a striking display. Mix red celosia or salvia, blue pansies or lobelia and yellow stock or marigolds; violet petunias, gold calendulas and dark green ivy; or pink geraniums, turquoise ageratum and yellow nasturtiums.

- **Foiled again.** Use white and neutrals, such as grey, to accent dark colors. Keep in mind that light-colored blooms look best against dark green foliage. Classic combinations, such as red geraniums and white petunias and white alyssum, coleus and dusty miller, fall into this category of using accents.

- **All in the family.** Using different shades within one color group is an easy and popular combination. Try rose, magenta and pink geraniums, or a proprietary blend of petunias or pansies for a tonal effect.

CHAPTER 7

Seasonal Promotions

FALL & HALLOWEEN

Ring Up Sales with Fall Promotions [1]

by Steven and Suz Trusty

Successful promotions are special happenings designed to bring bodies into your business—bodies that stay a while, enjoy interacting with things that interest them and buy something. They leave feeling good about the time they spent and the purchases they made. They have a reason to come back to shop at your place again.

Excitement is the key to successful promotions. "You've got to make people happy," says Jack Devitt, Devitt's Garden Center Inc., Newburgh, New York. "Your promotions have to stand out and say 'we're different.' They should separate you from the competition. You can do things, come up with promotions, without the most fantastic facility or the biggest store."

Pumpkins Make Good Business

Devitt's holds other promotions throughout the year, all of which display an individual style. For Halloween 1989, they built a stage and constructed a pumpkin-head band. These straw-filled characters wore old clothes, held actual old instruments and played into Indian corn microphones. A country and western tape played from underneath the platform. The dance floor at the front of the stage held two dancing pumpkin-head couples. Jack reports they knew they had a winner when several customers joined the pumpkin-head figures on the dance floor.

Try a Pumpkin Contest [2]

by Russell Miller

Jim and Jan Gulley started Gulley Greenhouse, Fort Collins, Colorado, in 1975. As a wholesale and retail operation, Gulley Greenhouse has been expanding rapidly over the years to meet a rising demand in the area for annuals and perennials, due mostly to the area's changing population characteristics.

About 20 schools tour Gulley Greenhouse in the spring. Jim and Jan give away pumpkin seed to the children, and in the fall, the children return with their pumpkins to enter a pumpkin contest with cash prizes. Some of the contests include the biggest pumpkin and smallest pumpkin, and for next year, the best carved Halloween pumpkin.

Pumpkins Help Sell Other Fall Crops [3]

by Russell Miller

Pumpkins are a profitable crop for Howard and Mary Ann Earsing, Earsing's Greenhouse, West Seneca, New York. With 8 acres of pumpkin field production, Earsing's pumpkin business is a retail niche that ties in nicely with hardy mums, flowering kale and other fall crops. "Pumpkins help sell other fall crops," Howard says. "One goes with the other. As customers shop for pumpkins, they are likely to pick up a hardy mum and vice versa."

The pumpkin selling season lasts 30 days in October, with the most activity occurring on weekends. Although they have never counted up all the pumpkins they sell during October, Howard estimates that on a good weekend they'll move at least 200 pumpkins a day. He estimates about 6 tons of pumpkins can be harvested from 1 acre of land.

One October, they nearly sold out of pumpkins. "People were looking for pumpkins earlier [that] year than they usually do," Howard says. "The selling season for pumpkins seems to be getting earlier."

Giving U-Pick an Incentive

"We allow our customers the choice between picking their own pumpkins from the field or choosing a pumpkin from our retail display area that we have picked," Howard says. Either way, pumpkins sell for the same price per pound. "Sales are about 50-50 between picking your own or choosing from the display area," he adds.

In the retail display areas, they also offer painted pumpkins and jack-o'lanterns for sale. They give customers ideas on what to do with the pumpkins after they get them home. "We also conduct pumpkin-carving demonstrations every day for school children and Boy Scout groups. During the demonstrations, the children are told how they can use what's left of the pumpkins—like baking the seeds—instead of throwing them out after the pumpkins are carved."

Picture a Spook

In Earsing's 4,000-square-foot outdoor retail display area, the benches used for displaying spring bedding plants are removed, and the space becomes a Halloween display area. Along the straw-covered floor you'll find a variety of witches and other Halloween figures that have the faces cut out so that customers can stand behind the figures, place their heads into the holes and have their pictures taken.

With a tractor and hay-filled trailer, Earsing's offers 30-minute hay rides out to the pumpkin field. "The hay ride is an adventure. It's very popular with the kids; they love it," Howard says. "We've had lines of people waiting for a hayride. Next year, we're thinking about taking the hay ride a step further and have Halloween displays out in the field."

FIGURE 19. *Pumpkin sales can complement other fall and early winter crops and novelty items such as gourds, corn stalks, clay jack-o-lanterns and forced paperwhite narcissus. Photo taken at Rudolph Galley, West Seneca, New York.*

157

October Floral Fairyland [4]

by Russell Miller

The most exciting yearly event at Molbak's in Woodinville, Washington, is their annual "October Floral Fairyland." Each year has a theme and this year's was "Little Red Riding Hood." Last year it was "Jack and the Beanstalk." Actors will perform 31 half-hour performances at Molbak's over three weekends—two on Friday, four on Saturday and four on Sunday—including one performance on Halloween.

"It's a Disneyland-style show," says Jerry Wilmot, former general manager. "We begin preparing for it in June, and by October we are ready to bring the stage props out of storage and present an entertaining performance. Usually, 200 people show up for each show.

"October isn't a big sales month for us, but the fairyland event is used to introduce the Christmas season to our customers. We have a different theme each year and always use plants as a unifying element. We don't look at this festival as providing us with an immediate payback. We are looking to build future, long-term customers.

"A lot of customers bring their children here to see the festival. In fact, some of our customers were first introduced to Molbak's as children when they took school tours of our greenhouses. Now they're bringing their children here, so a generation from now, we can expect these children to bring their children to Molbak's."

CHRISTMAS

Making Christmas a Success— Without Breaking Your Budget[5]

by Steven and Suz Trusty

Devitt's Garden Center, Newburgh, New York, is a family-owned business that started out serving the farm market in the early 1950s. By the end of the 1960s, as area farm land was sold out to residential development, the company had evolved into a lawn and garden, pet supply, power equipment, home needs center.

In the mid-1970s, the Devitts decided to tackle the Christmas business, and Jack Devitt traveled around to see what other people were doing. He found "lots of companies were spending lots of money to attract customers and were selling lots of merchandise. We wanted to attract that kind of traffic," says Jack.

Christmas on the Farm

The Devitts decided to create a Christmas promotion that would fit their limited budget. "We knew we wanted to put together something that would attract the kids, who would need to bring their parents with them.

"We had an empty greenhouse next to our showroom. We built pens and made trails and filled that greenhouse with an assortment of farm animals: goats, chickens, sheep, ducks, calves and pigs."

Thus was born "Christmas on the Farm." What Jack refers to as a "crude beginning" has developed into an area tradition. Newburgh is a community of 20,000. From November 1 through Christmas, Devitt's now draws from 70,000 to 75,000 people to the store.

Devitt's starts working on Christmas in July, when merchandise begins arriving and gets marked. Actual set-up starts around Labor Day, with the official opening November 1.

Bring the Country to the City

The central theme of Christmas on the Farm has also grown. "We were really surprised at what people didn't know about farm animals. The idea has advanced over the years into an educational program.

"Our people do background history on different topics, such as chickens. They tell people where white leghorns come from, and how

159

many eggs a chicken lays. We hatch chicks in an incubator. The 2-year-old child looks; the 12-year-old learns.

"We always have EGGbert, the talking egg, right up front. He's a 3-foot by 2-foot fiberglass shell, with moving eyes and mouth. An employee sits behind a two-way mirror and supplies the voice so EGGbert can talk to the kids. They love him.

"Petunia, our momma pig, helps out every year by having a litter of piglets around Thanksgiving. It's become part of the overall tradition," says Jack.

Devitt's has added animation as well as displays of decorated trees and Christmas merchandise. Shelves are covered and gazebos filled with cotton to show off decorations; frost-covered fencing displays wreaths. A poinsettia tower dominates a greenhouse. Everything is out of the bags and for sale. The Christmas on the Farm tour winds through these displays.

Becoming Part of a Tradition

"Our advertising urges people to bring the kids to see Christmas on the Farm. The husband is more likely to leave a football game on TV than he is to go Christmas shopping. The local papers feature us as part of the 'Traditions of the Hudson Valley.'

"We do a bit less paid advertising each year: some for the pre-season sale, then again the first three weeks in November and very little advertising beyond Thanksgiving. We actually spent more dollars on advertising in 1976 than in 1989.

FIGURE 20. *Entice customers away from the malls by offering unique and special Christmas items. This wreath was designed by Mo Halawi, Weidner's, Encinitas, California.*

"It took us five years to get the Christmas promotion off the ground, but we didn't spend a lot of money on things. We sold products, not just the sizzle, and it took some time. You have to have a goal, and take it step by step; it sure doesn't happen overnight," Jack says.

Doing Double Duty

Christmas opening is the second weekend in November. Whenever possible, the same basic structures are reworked to form the next story. Sometimes the structures and props are painted for Christmas and covered with cloth for Halloween. Then they are stripped and moved around to put together the Christmas story.

As people enter the garden center area from viewing the storyboards, they are handed a printed sheet of specials to "prime the pump." It encourages them to visit all areas of the garden center and make purchases.

Add a Christmas Shop [6]

by Ann Turner Whitman

Add a "second spring" to your garden center sales, give your staff a motivating pick-me-up, and keep your landscape workers employed during the off-season with savvy Christmas holiday marketing. It may be the most profitable move you ever make.

"Garden centers need to diversify just to keep going," says Elsa Duvendyke, owner of the 40-year-old family-run Dutch Growers Garden Centre in Saskatoon, Saskatchewan. "We used to sell only potted plants in the winter season," reports Elsa, but, since adding a Christmas shop in 1989, "Christmas is now our second busiest time of the year. Christmas is very profitable. It's our second spring."

"We started doing Christmas 20 years ago as a way to stay in the black at that time of year," agrees Wayne Holland, co-owner of Holland Gardens in Lubbock, Texas. "Christmas is 12 months of the year work, but we make more on Christmas than all the rest of the year," he says.

By mid-October, garden centers across the country undergo a seasonal transformation into fanciful and profitable Christmas shops. Glittering ornaments and blinking lights replace seeds and shrubs, while Santa holds court on a velvet-draped throne.

But adding a whole new line of merchandise can be daunting. Fresh-cut evergreens and artificial trees, collectibles and crafts, ribbons and garland plus a dazzling array of lights and ornaments await your buying decisions. How do you get started?

Survey Your Market

The first step, says Sally Dondis, owner of Greengate Garden Center in Lake Charles, Louisiana, is to survey your local market to see what other retailers are selling. "Travel is the key to success," agrees Sterling Cornelius, owner of Cornelius Nurseries in Houston, Texas. "Travel in the height of the season to see what others are doing. Most people are willing to share information with independents. You need to expose yourself to others and pick what suits your demographic area."

After visiting other shops, "decide how you want to go into it," Sally continues. Do you want to sell just fresh trees and wreaths, or do you plan to offer artificial, too? How much storage space can you devote to lights, garlands and glass ornaments? Do you plan to offer craft items or collectibles?

"Determine the price point you want to pursue, and do a business plan," she advises. "Stay away from mass-merchandised products. Medium to expensive items usually sell best for Christmas shops."

"We started doing Christmas in 1961 and failed miserably because we bought the wrong merchandise at first. We had to find our market," admits Sterling. "You have to be unique to compete with the mass merchandisers who have buyers in the Orient. You have to be very selective."

Trade Shows Are a Starting Point

Select your merchandise at seasonal shows and permanent showrooms. The buying season starts in January. Although Dale Black, buyer for Cornelius, cautions that "trade shows can be mind-boggling," she advises visiting them as well as show rooms, which set up in major cities throughout the country, to see how products are featured and displayed. "Display is what sells the merchandise," says Dale.

Decorating starts in early August at Holland Gardens. The staff looks forward to the end of the garden season when they can begin setting up for Christmas, says Wayne. They like the fresh new look of the store, but, after a few months of it, they are anxious to get back into the gardening season. "We get two pick-me-ups a year," he says. "It's a real motivator."

Offer Unique Services and Products

"You have to entice customers away from the malls, give them a reason to make a special trip," says Elsa Duvendyke. Located on the frigid Canadian plains, Dutch Growers Garden Centre offers something unique: an indoor forest of Christmas trees. They hang the fresh-cut trees from bungee straps inside their greenhouses to thaw and open their branches so customers can shop in comfort. The trees sell well, especially in cold winters, Elsa reports.

In Texas, where warmer holiday weather prevails, Cornelius Nurseries sells their fresh-cut trees on sealed watered stands. Customers receive a $10 to $12 rebate when they return the stand after Christmas.

Premium trees also help differentiate them from competing tree lots. Cornelius only sells Noble and Frasier firs with some Douglas fir and blue spruce by special order. "Live trees are a great end of our business now that we've stopped doing Scotch pine," says Sterling.

The nursery also offers tree delivery for $25, which includes pick-up after the holidays. A great way to use off-season landscape labor!

High-quality artificial trees are also taking hold for several reasons, reports Sterling. The quality has gone up, and the price has come down. Many people are allergic to live trees or have environmental concerns. Artificial trees cost customers more up front, but "they make up the cost in three or four years," he says. Cornelius offers 75 different sizes and styles.

Up with the Lights

Garden center owners who want to break into Christmas marketing gradually might start with a lighting service, recommends Wayne Holland. He keeps his landscape crew busy putting up and taking down outdoor lights for their regular clients.

His staff also teaches customers how to permanently attach lights to their artificial trees and offers a professional lighting service (10 cents per bulb) for customers who don't want to do it themselves.

A miniature train winds its way through a snowy scene right out of a Charles Dickens' Christmas story, courtesy of Bachman's Department 56, a series of collectible figures. At Revay's Garden and Gift Shop in East Windsor, Connecticut, the year-round gift and Christmas shop accounts for 50 percent of their sales, reports owner Francis Revay.

In addition to Department 56, his shop offers Swarovski Austrian crystal, Byer's Choice and many other lines of china, crystal, porcelain and pewter collectible items. He sends customers postcards and newsletters to keep them informed of special showings, silent auctions and other events related to their collecting hobby.

Lights, Color, Action!

Animated woodland creatures celebrate the season among waterfalls and snowy evergreens in winter twilight at Revay's. Each year, a section of their retail greenhouse becomes magically transformed into the Enchanted Forest, a tourist destination as well as a traditional holiday attraction for families in surrounding towns.

Children especially enjoy Teddy the Talking Tree. "[Animation] excites the children, which excites the parents," agrees Wayne Holland. Holland Gardens uses about 150 animated pieces, he says.

At the center of most Christmas shops' merchandising effort lies intensively decorated artificial "theme" trees. "We do about a dozen theme trees," says Dale Black at Cornelius. "We use some animated stuff. Customers can walk from one theme to another. Each theme is complete."

Themes Appeal

Holland Gardens decorates as many as 80 theme trees. Half of these are set up on slowly revolving turntables made from 4- to 8-foot-diameter wire spools decorated with craft paper and fabric. Theme possibilities are endless. Retailers may use brass, crystal, sports, music, Victoriana, nature, pets, angels, Disney characters, Santa, Ireland, Russia, careers, the circus and many other themes to sell individual ornaments and complete packages.

For wide-ranging appeal, retailers look beyond red, green and white color themes. "Color is very important," says Wayne Holland. "We use fashion colors as well as traditional [Christmas colors]. Look at carpet and furniture samples to coordinate Christmas decorations," he advises. Up-scale customers especially want their Christmas selections to harmonize with their home decor.

Special Events

Use craft fairs, open houses, tours, charity benefits, seminars and petting zoos to attract customers to your store. Christmas open house, held the second or third weekend in October, is a very big event for Holland Gardens.

"The sooner we do an open house, the sooner we get selling," says Wayne. "Our more affluent customers shop early so that they have time to coordinate their Christmas look." Holland Gardens flies in some fresh cut trees from Oregon to add fragrance and festivity. They also have gift certificate giveaways and offer special prices on holiday items.

At Dutch Growers, from mid-summer until early spring, half the retail store is devoted to crafts. They offer free craft seminars three times a week that are so popular that often all 50 spaces in each class will be reserved within days of the offering. Subjects include stenciling, dried floral baskets, wreath-making and folk art painting. Customers buy their supplies at the store.

Crafts, Tours Bring in Customers

Retailers who don't want to get into the craft business but still want to profit from its popularity may consider leasing space to exhibitors for a craft show. Vicki Walker, manager of Black's Nursery in El Paso, Texas, says craft show organizers bring in 50 artisans to sell their wares in the nursery's barn. The show attracts crowds of potential customers.

Tours are another way to bring in customers. Holland Gardens organized a program for self-guided school bus tours. Teachers come in before the tour to pick up a program and map and schedule an arrival time for their students. Wayne reports that this system works well because he doesn't need extra staff to guide the tours.

FIGURE 21. *When planning your Christmas displays, don't forget to include attractions and activities for children. Photo by Adrian Keating, Vernon, Connecticut.*

He encourages teachers to come early in the day and asks children to hold hands while in the store. Last year, 97 busloads of children came from surrounding towns to visit his animated displays.

Don't Forget to Give

Charity events, especially at the holidays, bring good will as well as good customers to your garden center. Revay's donates proceeds from several events to charity. They sponsor a special breakfast with Santa, stage photo opportunities with Santa and hold an auction of collectibles.

Ellison's Greenhouses in Brenham, Texas, holds a huge poinsettia celebration on Thanksgiving weekend in conjunction with a local non-profit organization. All proceeds go to non-profit groups while Ellison's enjoys the publicity.

Hamlen's Garden Center in Swanton, Vermont, offers a petting zoo for youngsters who may be bored with Mom's Christmas shopping. Santa's pet sheep and goats come to live in the greenhouse where children can feed and pet them.

Commit to Christmas

"Don't start too small," advises Elsa Duvendyke. "You won't get the impact, the traffic draw. You have to entice customers away from the malls, give them a reason to make a special trip," she says.

"Commitment is important. If you really commit yourself to Christmas, sales of plants and fall stuff will increase, too," says Dale Black. "Get into it," adds Sterling. "Don't say it's too much trouble; you can't afford not to diversify. December has changed from our No. 12 month into our No. 1 month in gross volume."

"Christmas done right can be the most profitable time of the year," agrees Wayne Holland.

DISPLAY GARDENS

Display Ideas for Super Sales [7]

by Steven and Suz Trusty

Consumers are always looking for quality plant materials. You grow 'em, so show 'em! Triangular plant beds at Rogers Gardens, Corona Del Mar, California, fill a hillside between an upper and lower walkway.

Each section is planted with one variety. Each is marked by name and growth characteristics on signs that can be easily read from either direction. Flats of the material are located nearby, either beside the bed or across the walkway, and items are priced.

- The effect of a mass display is tremendous. Featuring any plant material in such a section greatly boosts its sales. The beds are changed frequently, both to add to the showplace effect and to sell different items.

- Rogers Gardens sells hanging baskets in all shapes and forms, and displays them throughout the entire sales area.

- Display related hardgoods as well as plant material. A massive showing of clay and decorative pots encourages add-on sales. The customer benefits by getting all of the items needed to complete a project; you benefit from the extra profits.

- Accentuate the positive atmosphere of your business. Colonial Nursery Inc., Blue Springs, Missouri, greets each shopper with a landscaped area complete with bird feeders and spring flowering bulbs, extending from the parking lot to the entrance and continuing along the side of the building.

- The Barn, Olympia, Washington, features several display beds devoted to annuals and perennials that make lovely cut flower arrangements. Customers can observe the plants' growth habits throughout the season to determine which varieties they will add to their own planting areas.

Whenever plants are blooming, shoppers are free to borrow a pruning shear, take a mason jar and cut their own bouquets. The small fee is much less than that of a prepared floral arrangement, and the variety is greater than that found in most home gardens. Customers return again and again to select from seasonally changing bloomers and nearly always purchase additional items during their visits.

Trial Gardens and an Open House Team Up for Sales [8]

by Peter Konjoian

During the last several years, I'm sure you've witnessed the proliferation of plant cultivars that are being offered by plant and seed companies. Most of the new material is exciting, but putting too many new cultivars into the production without adequate display area and merchandising effort can cause much confusion.

At Konjoian Greenhouses, Andover, Massachusetts, we have about 1,500 square feet of display area for the 7,000 flats of bedding plants we produce. That's quite tight. This area is turned over about seven times during the bedding plant season.

FIGURE 22. *Specialty displays like this array of herbs can spur off-season sales. Photo taken at Southern Homes and Gardens, Montgomery, Alabama.*

We cannot display more than six flats of any cultivar and most often display fewer. Constant stocking and tending is required, which keeps us right there with the customers.

Potted plants are retailed similarly, with about 50,000 pots sold through a display area of about 5,000 square feet. Hanging baskets are displayed in both sales areas and receive the same attention as bedding and potted plants with regard to stocking.

Gardens Take Time and Effort

It takes little space to create trial gardens around your greenhouses. We started ours to have living proof for our summer customers that flowers really do last all season long with proper care. We also use the gardens to trial new offerings and help make production decisions. With all the cultivars available, outdoor trials provide valuable information.

A word of caution is necessary, however, because the gardens take a lot of effort and care. If you don't have the time to tend them, the idea could backfire, resulting in poorly kept beds that fail to impress anyone. Spend some money on drip irrigation, and tap into your constant feed lines in the greenhouse to help out.

Show off your garden at an open house during mid- to late summer. Publicize it and have refreshments and maybe even a door prize or raffle to make it exciting. Use it to show some new design ideas or color schemes. Encourage people to make notes for next year and have cultivars labeled clearly. Then keep your fingers crossed for good weather!

Displays Create Year-round Sales [9]

by C. Anne Whealy

"From a retail merchandising aspect, people like to wander through greenhouses and buy from a grower," says Frans Peters, Humber Greenhouses, Brampton, Ontario. "People will come here in January, February and March just to watch everything grow. Growing really appeals to people, and it makes them want to come back. Seventy percent of our customers are repeat, 20 percent are word of mouth and the other 10 percent come from advertising."

Special Days Draw Customers

For promotions, Humber offers a "pak" of the week, Ladies' Day on Wednesdays and Senior Citizens' Day on Thursdays. Wednesdays at Cullen Country Barns, Markham, Ontario, is 10 percent off on bedding plants for everybody.

The details of effective display are important to both retailers. Time is spent replacing plants to make full packs, arranging colors attractively, keeping varieties straight and maintaining an orderly display. Raised benches are used so that nothing is displayed on the ground.

At Humber the production greenhouses are the display greenhouses, and they have several outdoor display areas. "We have a perennial trial area for new products. If they perform well and we like them, then we'll sell them. People like to come and see what these plants will look like in the landscape," says Frans.

"When we display baskets, we have a lot of 5-inch nearby so they can make their own. We make displays in the building, too, because not everyone wants to walk down through the greenhouses. For instance, we'll bring in some tomato plants, cages, stakes and fertilizers," he adds.

OPEN HOUSES

Open to the Public [10]

by Neal Catapano

Don't underestimate the value of your growing facility as a selling point. People love going into greenhouses, seeing the plants, smelling the dirt and feeling the humidity. At Catapano Farms in Southold, New York, our entire growing facility is fully open to the retail public every day.

As people enter our range, their eyes widen in amazement as they see literally millions of bedding plants or thousands of poinsettias. We don't realize that the beauty we see every day is absolutely dumbfounding to the average person.

Give People a Reason to Shop Here

Flowers and flower growing have an inherent charm that can give us an advantage over the mass marketers in the customers' minds; our greenhouses can make them taste and smell the season like no other experience.

Finally, most customers are just plain looking for good reasons to shop at a locally owned family business. Let's make sure they have plenty. Properly managed, growing and retailing flowers can continue to provide a good living and a wonderful way of life well into the future.

A Barbeque in the Garden [11]

by Dawn Nelson

At Stutzman Greenhouse in Hutchinson, Kansas, Ben Miller operates a 5-acre growing and retail facility. Like others in this industry his company attends and exhibits at trade shows each year. They also conduct mini seminars at a local hotel and invite store buyers to attend. The sessions are structured for small groups and address concerns, answer questions and share information.

"In effect, we become an extension service for our customers," says Ben. It sounds simple, but customer relations is often an overlooked part of marketing and good public relations. "We listen to our customers," he says.

171

About five times a year Stutzman plans a promotion that ties in with local supermarkets' special events. Ben also frequently tests plants to see what will hold up well in Kansas' scorching heat. Each year his nursery plants a 1-acre test garden of annuals and perennials. This garden is also the location for a barbeque for special guests.

Don't Overlook Garden Clubs, Guided Tours

Ben encourages his customers to stay in touch with their end-users. He does this by working with garden clubs and park departments, giving them new varieties of plants to use. He also takes 2,000 to 3,000 children on guided tours of the greenhouse to witness the seeding process. Ben wants to expose children to the beauty and joy of gardening at an early age.

Once a year Stutzman supplies its customers with a computer printout of materials they've purchased and used successfully. Ben admits that motivation for these positive PR moves comes from seeing satisfaction on customers' faces. "The more you work with your customers, the more enthusiastic and successful they become," he says.

At year's end Ben anticipates he will have spent about $8,000 for these extra activities. He says, "It's a commitment. People remember what we do in this community. That counts for a lot."

Ben believes that one of the most important things his nursery can do is to produce a superior product. "If we don't, our customers will become discouraged and spend that disposable income in some other way."

GIVEAWAYS & DISCOUNTS

"Moose Bucks" Work [12]

by Kathleen Pyle

In St. Catharine's, the "Garden City" of Ontario, Canada, bedding plants are big business and Broadway Gardens' foundation, says Jerry Moes Sr., who owns the 26-year-old retail/wholesale operation, but has handed over the greenhouse's day-to-day management to his sons, Jerry Jr. and Rob.

"Moose Bucks" Bring Customers Back

With a plant product mix geared to support the garden center with year-round color, the Moes also work at strengthening the retail focus with promotions. They grow 9,000 poinsettias for Christmas retail sales. Broadway Gardens' two-day Christmas open house, held at the end of November, combines a 50-vendor craft show with the holiday sales kickoff and draws about 1,000 visitors per day, the Moes estimate.

For over 10 years "Moose Bucks" have been a Broadway Gardens' tradition. An idea picked up from a Canadian Tires' promotion, they are coupons entitling customers to 5 percent off their next purchase. According to Jerry Jr., shoppers redeem over $25,000 in "Moose Bucks" each year.

Senior Citizen Specials Work [13]

by Julie A. Martens

Add together an advertising campaign, extended spring business hours—open daily until 8 p.m. from April 15 to July 1—an 800 number, a traffic director, an army of cashiers and Senior Citizen Specials held on Monday each week, and you've got the formula for retail success at Claussen's Florist & Greenhouse, Colchester, Vermont.

Weekends at the Colchester site create tricky traffic patterns. The garden center sits on a two-lane city street one block past a busy intersection; traffic jams are an hourly event. Owner-manger Chris Conant tackled this problem by offering special senior citizen discounts on Monday, using maintenance personnel to direct cars, and extending business hours.

Retailing Ideas for Super Sales [14]

by Steven and Suz Trusty

Promotions, such as the R. Good Customer Discount Card offered by The Greenery, Omaha, Nebraska, are designed to encourage repeat business. Many variations may be devised to achieve the desired results.

A discount can be given at each visit when the good customer card is shown. A card can be punched for each purchase, earning a discount or free goods when a certain plateau is reached. Coupons can be given at one season for free goods at another, such as a coupon for a dozen free tulips with a $10 purchase of bedding plants.

Most such promotions more than pay for themselves in the additional sales generated, but until you have established a financial history of each event's costs and returns, it's best for budgeting purposes to allocate all costs as advertising expense.

Free with Purchase [15]

by Julie A. Martens

Tierra Vista Inc. started in 1984 from a well-known lawn maintenance company in Tulsa, Oklahoma. They got into greenhouse growing in a big way, producing year-round color from plugs to finished product. In a *GrowerTalks* interview, greenhouse manager Kelly Keetch answered some questions about promotions.

Promotions, Image Building

What's been your most successful promotion?

"Garden trowels with a Tierra Vista sticker on them. We first offered them free with every $15 purchase; now they go with every $25 purchase. We gave away 8,000 this year. Our investment in them is only 50 cents."

What are your future promotion plans? Anything special?

"I'm working to create an image of Tierra Vista in people's minds. I want people to think of us as their total retail source—for plants, for hardgoods, for information.

"I've contracted with a local radio personality to run broadcasts at the greenhouses, highlighting a crop and the things that happen in growing a crop to raise public awareness of growing and of the company.

"Image building doesn't happen overnight; it will be a long-term effect. The way I see it, though, we've already got advertising out there for us in the 52 lawn maintenance trucks. When people see those, I want them to think of the retail store on 51st Street."

Put a New Twist on the Old "Sale" [16]

by Russell Miller

Bernardin's Florist, Garden Center & Landscaping is a 32,000-square-foot operation in Mokena, Illinois, about 30 miles southwest of downtown Chicago.

"We're very customer-service oriented," Rick Bernardin says. "We're always coming up with different promotions and gimmicks to get new customers and increase repeat business. Some of our ideas may not be moneymakers, but they do provide for good PR."

Service and Education Are Key

In addition to one-on-one customer service provided by the staff, there are also about 15 to 20 information pamphlets and handouts at the front retail counter for the customers to take home. Bernardin's also prints its own information book filled with gardening information covering a wide range of subjects.

This spring they took four boxes of fiber half-flats they found stored away in the attic. They filled these with 36 plants each and sold them for $3.75, as long as a customer also bought $5 of additional hard goods. "We called it 'Grandpa's Old-Fashioned Flat Sale,' and referred to it as a 20-year price roll-back," Cathy Sanchez, greenhouse manager, says.

They also promoted "The Child's Garden," 15 easy-to-grow and care-for vegetables and flowering plants in a fiber flat that sells for $5.95. In the fall, children can come back and receive a free pumpkin with a coupon given with the flat.

Live Insects On Display

This spring Cathy used plastic florist containers to display live specimens of cicadas and tent caterpillars on the front counter. "The response from the customers is very interesting," Rick says. "Some walk by, come to a dead stop at the display and say, 'That's what I have in my tree. What do I do?' It gives us another opportunity to educate a customer."

Two-for-One [17]

by Russell Miller

"We do a quarterly newsletter and a lot of public relations," Egon Molbak, of Molbak's Greenhouse in Wodinville, Washington, says. Public relations takes the form of contributions, and Molbak's donates or sells plants and hard goods to businesses and non-profit charities.

"We do a lot of contributions, I mean a lot," Egon says. "However, we aren't much for specials or discount sales."

An entire crop is grown for their one big bedding plant sale held every year during the first two weeks of July. This is a "two-for-one" sale, but it isn't used to sell leftover plant material. "We grow for this sale," Egon says. "We have between 200 and 300 people here standing in line before the store opens on the first day of the sale."

"During those two weeks, we move 60 percent more plant material than we do on our biggest week in May, which is our biggest sales volume month of the year," says Roger Luce, production manager. Two other significant sales held during the year are a January Green Sale and a September "Back to Houseplants" sale.

Bibliography

All articles orginally appeared in *GrowerTalks* magazine with one exception as noted. Minor editorial changes have been incorporated.

CHAPTER 1 Make Space for Retailing

1. "Plan for Success When Planning Garden Center Changes," Steven and Suz Trusty, May 1989.
2. "Space—the Retailer's Frontier," Dave Hamlen, March 1992.
3. "To Park or Not to Park: the Springtime Challenge," Dave Hamlen, April 1992.
4. "Busy Bee Greenhouses—Quality Plants and a Whole Lot More," Russell Miller, November 1989.
5. "Making a Long-term Investment in Retail," Julie A. Martens, November 1992.
6. From "Moving Plants—and More—at a One-Stop-Shopping Retail Center," Julie A. Martens, June 1990.
7. "Molbak's of Seattle: We Are Retail-Driven," Russell Miller, September 1988.
8. From "Under an Acre" department, Russell Miller, April 1989.
9. From "Under an Acre" department, Julie A. Martens, February 1990.
10. "Ideas That Ring Up Sales," Steven and Suz Trusty, May 1991.

CHAPTER 2 Plan Your Product Mix

1. From "Under an Acre" department, Julie A. Martens, August 1992.
2. From "Under an Acre" department, Julie A. Martens, February 1993.
3. From "Under an Acre" department, Kathleen Pyle, August 1991.
4. From "Marketing in the 1990s—Customer Service Is Where It's At," Peter Konjoian, June 1990.
5. From "Under an Acre" department, Julie A. Martens, October 1990.
6. From "Georgia Perennials: a Retail Success," Julie A. Martens, June 1993.
7. From "Moving Plants—and More—at a One-Stop-Shopping Retail Center," Julie A. Martens, June 1990.
8. From "Under an Acre" department, Russell Miller, December 1990.
9. From "Under an Acre" department, Julie A. Martens, September 1991.

CHAPTER 3 Color Bowls and Containers

1. "Extend Your Season and Your Cash Flow with Color Bowls and Containers," Ann Turner Whitman, January 1990.
2. "Combo Planters Are Hot Sellers for the '90s," Ann Turner Whitman, March 1991.

3. "Discover the Profit Potential in Color Bowls," Ann Turner Whitman, January 1993.
4. From "Niche Marketing at Niche Gardens," Kim Hawks, October 1989.
5. From "Under an Acre" department, Julie A. Martens, August 1990.
6. From "Under an Acre" department, Russell Miller, November 1990.
7. From "Under an Acre" department, Julie A. Martens, April 1991.
8. From "Retailing in a Competitive Environment: the Grower-Retailer's Advantage," Neal Catapano, February 1993.

CHAPTER 4 Employee Management

1. "You Can Become a Better Employee Manager," Steven and Suz Trusty, November 1989.
2. "14 Ways to Get and Keep Good Employees," Russell Miller, January 1989.
3. From "How to Avoid Mutiny in the Greenhouse," Dave Hamlen, August 1992.
4. "Getting the Most from Your No. 1 Resource—Employees," John H. Saxtan, May 1989.
5. From "Making Family Business Work—Beyond Bloodlines," Julie A. Martens, October 1991.
6. From "Molbak's of Seattle: We Are Retail Driven," Russell Miller, September 1988.
7. From "Selling Out in an Economic Slowdown," Julie A. Martens, November 1991.
8. From "155 Acres of Customer Service at Campbell's," Russell Miller, February 1989.

CHAPTER 5 Customer Service

1. "Customer Satisfaction: Make Serving Customers Your Organization's Driving Force," Ivan C. Smith, February 1993.
2. "Use Surveys to Define and Measure Retail Customer Satisfaction," Ivan C. Smith, October 1992.
3. From "155 Acres of Customer Service at Campbell's," Russell Miller, February 1989.
4. From "Retailing in a Competitive Environment: the Grower-Retailer's Advantage," Neal Catapano, February 1993.
5. From "Customer Service Is the King in the '90s," Ann Turner Whitman, February 1991.
6. From "Wholesale-Gone-Retail Means Better Profits," Julie A. Martens, December 1991.
7. From "Marketing in the 1990s—Customer Service Is Where It's At," Peter Konjoian, June 1990.
8. "Pleasing Mrs. Persnickety," Dave Hamlen, October 1992.
9. From "Retailing Ideas for Super Sales," Steven and Suz Trusty, January 1989.
10. From "Under an Acre" department, Julie A. Martens, May 1991.

CHAPTER 6   Marketing

1. From "Wholesale-Gone-Retail Means Better Profits," Julie A. Martens, December 1991.
2. From "Under an Acre" department, Russell Miller, April 1989.
3. From "Marketing in the 1990s—Customer Service Is Where It's At," Peter Konjoian, June 1990.
4. From "155 Acres of Customer Service at Campbell's," Russell Miller, February 1989.
5. From "Under an Acre" department, Kathleen Pyle, November 1989.
6. From "Under an Acre" department, Russell Miller, August 1988.
7. From "Making Family Business Work—Beyond Bloodlines," Julie A. Martens, October 1991.
8. From "It Pays to Advertise," Roy A. Larson, October 1991.
9. From "Under an Acre" department, Russell Miller, November 1988.
10. From "Under an Acre" department, Julie A. Martens, May 1989.
11. "Targeting Your Customers with Direct Mail Part 3: How to Choose a List for Successful Direct Mailing," Mary Lu Parks, December 1988.
12. From "Metro Toronto: Boom Town for Bedding," C. Anne Whealy, October 1988.
13. "Providing Gardening Solutions Keeps Customers Coming Back," Douglas Green, Octoboer 1990.
14. From "Under an Acre" department, Russell Miller, April 1989.
15. From "Selling Out in an Economic Slowdown," Julie A. Martens, November 1991.
16. From "Metro Toronto: Boom Town for Bedding," C. Anne Whealy, October 1988.
17. From "Under an Acre" department, Julie A. Martens, January 1990.
18. From "Under an Acre" department, Russell Miller, July 1990.
19. From "Increase Sales with Community Goodwill," Dawn Nelson, August 1992.
20. "Marketing—What It Is and How to Do It," Ivan C. Smith, July 1991.
21. "Practical Ways to Discover and Serve Your Niche Market," Steven and Suz Trusty, June 1990.
22. "Cash in on Environmental Marketing," Ann Turner Whitman, September 1992.
23. "Merchandising: the Art of Profitable Persuasion," John H. Saxtan, December 1987.
24. "What Color Are Your Sales?" John H. Saxtan, October 1988.
25. From "Successful Color Combinations," Ann Turner Whitman, July 1992.

CHAPTER 7   Seasonal Promotions

1. From "Ring up Sales with Promotions That Work," Steven and Suz Trusty, June 1990.
2. From "Under an Acre" department, Russell Miller, December 1990.
3. From "Under an Acre" department, Russell Miller, January 1991.
4. From "Molbak's of Seattle: We Are Retail-Driven," Russell Miller, September 1988.

5. From "Ring up Sales with Promotions That Work," Steven and Suz Trusty, June 1990.
6. "Add a Christmas Shop," Ann Turner Whitman, written for *GrowerTalks on Retailing*.
7. From "Retailing Ideas for Super Sales," Steven and Suz Trusty, January 1989.
8. From "Marketing in the 1990s: Customer Service Is Where It's At," Peter Konjoian, June 1990.
9. From "Metro Toronto: Boom Town for Bedding," C. Anne Whealy, October 1988.
10. From "Retailing in a Competitive Environment: the Grower-Retailer's Advantage," Neal Catapano, February 1993.
11. From "Increase Sales with Community Goodwill," Dawn Nelson, August 1992.
12. From "Under an Acre" department, Kathleen Pyle, December 1991.
13. From "Making Family Business Work—Beyond Bloodlines," Julie A. Martens, October 1991.
14. From "Retailing Ideas for Super Sales," Steven and Suz Trusty, January 1989.
15. From "Wholesale-Gone-Retail Means Better Profits," Julie A. Martens, December 1991.
16. From "Under an Acre" department, Russell Miller, July 1990.
17. From "Molbak's of Seattle: We Are Retail-Driven," Russell Miller, September 1988.

Index